PRAISE FOR
TOE TO TOE WITH YOUR TEEN

This is a very hopeful book. Dr. Myers gives you excellent understanding and the tools to cope with your defiant teenager. It's part teenager training and part parenting school.

JIM BURNS
Author, *Confident Parenting, Creating an Intimate Marriage*
and *Teaching Your Children Healthy Sexuality*
President, HomeWord, San Juan Capistrano, California

Inspirational. Practical. Biblically sound. Culturally relevant and funny. Need help raising a defiant teen? This book is for you!

DR. TIM CLINTON
President of the American Association of Christian Counselors, Forest, Virginia

What Jimmy Myers lays out in this book is accurate and right on the money. The material is captivating and reads easily, and the Christian perspective and biblical insights provide hope and comfort. Jimmy's lighthearted style and humor makes the sometimes harsh reality of raising a difficult teen easier to swallow.

MARTHA D.
Parent of a Defiant Teen

In my years of youth ministry, I have talked with many parents whose teenagers have seemed to morph into extremely defiant "strangers." They feel confused and guilty, and their pain is intense. I am so grateful that I can recommend this helpful resource to these parents. It is practical, thorough and, above all, hopeful. I believe it can begin real change.

DOUG FIELDS
President, Simply Youth Ministry
Orange County, California

Most parents who would pick up a book like this on parenting are in one of two situations: Either they are close to the edge with a child who seems "too far gone" and feel that their efforts in parenting have failed, or they feel they are relatively healthy but are open to new ways of looking at family issues. I would put this book in the hands of these parents and any others who are interested in a biblical, relational and loving family.

DR. R. ALLEN JACKSON
Director of the Youth Ministry Institute, New Orleans Seminary
New Orleans, Louisiana

Dr. Myers has penned one of the best books of its kind for demoralized parents of behaviorally defiant teenagers. Parents and professionals alike will find fresh insights, empowering strategies and clinically sound step-by-step instructions for navigating the turbulent waters of raising non-compliant teens. Cemented in biblical truth, clinical experience and research, this work is a must-read. I strongly recommend it to my own clients.

JOHN C. THOMAS, PH.D.
Director of the Ph.D. Program, Center for Counseling and
Family Studies, Liberty University, Lynchburg, Virginia
Author, *What's Good About Feeling Bad: Finding Purpose and a Path Through Suffering*

JIMMY MYERS, Ph.D.

TOE TO TOE

WITH YOUR TEEN

A GUIDE TO

SUCCESSFULLY PARENTING A DEFIANT TEEN WITHOUT GIVING UP OR GIVING IN

Regal

From Gospel Light
Ventura, California, U.S.A.

Published by Regal
From Gospel Light
Ventura, California, U.S.A.
www.regalbooks.com
Printed in the U.S.A.

Library of Congress Cataloging-in-Publication Data
Myers, Jimmy.
Toe-to-toe with your teen : successfully parenting a defiant teen
without giving up or giving in / Jimmy Myers.
p. cm.
ISBN 978-0-8307-4901-0 (trade paper)
1. Parent and teenager—Religious aspects—Christianity. 2. Parenting—Religious
aspects—Christianity. 3. Child rearing—Religious aspects—Christianity. I. Title.
BV4529.M95 2009
248.8'45—dc22
2009010048

2 3 4 5 6 7 8 9 10 11 12 13 14 15 / 15 14 13 12 11 10

Rights for publishing this book outside the U.S.A. or in non-English languages are
administered by Gospel Light Worldwide, an international not-for-profit ministry.
For additional information, please visit www.glww.org, email info@glww.org, or write
to Gospel Light Worldwide, 1957 Eastman Avenue, Ventura, CA 93003, U.S.A.

I would like to dedicate this book to Bill and Sybil Myers,
my parents. They taught me so much about life, love and
family before I even realized I was learning.
And to the greatest parent I've ever had a chance to witness,
my wife, Beth. In spite of me, her natural wisdom, love, encouragement,
patience and protectiveness produced the three greatest children
the world has ever known.

CONTENTS

FOREWORD

I cannot tell you how much I appreciate this outstanding book by Jimmy Myers. It should be read by all parents, not simply those with behaviorally difficult teens. I say this because it is full of profound guidance and advice useful to parents of children of any age.

I also respect this book because it discusses a critical area that few other parenting books cover: the culture in which we find ourselves. There is no doubt that this is the most difficult period in our nation's history in which to raise children. I know of no other time in world history in which a culture has produced such an epidemic of disturbed teenagers. I am so thankful to Jimmy Myers for writing this book. It is just what the doctor ordered to help parents caught in this unbelievably difficult situation.

Until recently, we could say, "Even though our culture is on a downhill spiral, we parents and grandparents still have the greatest influence on our children and teens." Tragically, in most cases, the culture now has the greater influence today. This cultural influence is becoming more and more unhealthy, and increasingly evil. Violence, drugs, pregnancy, sexually transmitted diseases, abortion, suicide and even homicide have become commonplace. This is indeed a different world than it was a short time ago. It is therefore critical that parents and grandparents understand this new culture and protect our children and teenagers from its negative influences. Otherwise, our precious ones will become part of it and not have a strong moral rudder to guide them.

Tragically, most parents do not realize how our nation's culture has changed and do not know how to cope with it. Jimmy Myers does a masterful job in making this complex area more understandable to parents who read this book. How I pray that today's parents will allow themselves to be educated regarding this radical shift and learn to protect their dear ones from it. Let's face it: We need all the help we can get in this "brave, new world," and this book is a wonderful aid. I am grateful for it.

Another factor that makes *Toe to Toe with Your Teen* so unique is the spiritual content that Dr. Myers includes. I am deeply impressed with the ways he uses Scripture to illustrate and strengthen the many teachings he offers. Dr. Myers has counseled in these critical areas for 30 years, and it is obvious that he lives what he writes and advocates.

One positive characteristic you will find in reading this book is how thoroughly Jimmy Myers covers topics such as anger, guilt, appropriate and inappropriate trust, leadership, parent control and the connection between behavior and relationship. There is a tremendous amount of vital material in this well-written book, and I strongly recommend that you keep it in a handy place and reread it on occasion, especially when your relationship with your child does not feel right.

Most parents of teenagers are hurting, confused and fearful of the future, and it is my hope and prayer that this book becomes widespread throughout the country. It is needed by every parent.

D. Ross Campbell, M.D.
Associate professor of pediatrics and psychiatry
College of Medicine, University of Tennessee
Author of *How to Really Love Your Teenager, How to Really
    Parent Your Teenager,* and other books on parenting

INTRODUCTION

WINNING THE WAR ON TERROR

This book is not your typical collection of Christian principles for parenting adolescents. The bookstore shelves are full of wonderful books on that subject by such authors as Dr. James Dobson, Paul David Tripp and Ross Campbell, M.D., just to name a few. During the past 30 years of working with teenagers and their families, I've read most, if not all, of those parenting books. I've taught from them, recommended them and benefited personally from many of them.

However, the book you're about to read is quite different, and the differences may be striking. This is because I'm not writing to the parent who is looking for a more engaging home devotional for their teen, or to the parents who are seeking ways to get their child to help out more around the house.

Instead, I'll be sharing what I've learned while working with a particular type of teenager and their parents. You may find some of their stories disturbing. You may believe my tone is at times inappropriately harsh or the proposed strategies too extreme. If so, I can certainly understand where you're coming from. However, I believe you picked up this book for a reason. Chances are the reason is that your child is one of the estimated six million teenagers who could be considered exceptionally defiant. Your home is one of the estimated three million homes affected by the constant turmoil and agitation that comes with raising an exceptionally defiant teen. If so, this book is designed for you: the parent whose life has been turned upside down by an exceptionally defiant teenager and who longs for a return to normalcy.

The Adolescent Defiance Scale

So what constitutes an exceptionally defiant teenager? Someone may say, "My child rolled her eyes at me this morning when I told her we were going to visit her grandmother this weekend. Is that what you're talking about?" While those typical self-centered teen attitudes can be frustrating, that is not the type of behavior to which I'm referring. Someone else might say, "My child snuck out last night and we had to pick him up at the police station, where he was charged with 'minor in possession.' Is that what you're talking about?" Bless your heart. Yes, now we're zeroing in on the type of defiant behavior that will be addressed in the following pages.

Later on, we will spend one whole chapter examining ways you can determine if your child's behavior warrants serious concern, but I thought we could begin here by putting some numbers to it. Take a look at the defiance scale drawn below, and then consider the related behavioral descriptions to determine just how defiant your child's behavior actually is.

Adolescent Defiance Scale (ADS)

Normal Teen Behavior	Defiant Teen	Extremely Defiant Teen	Criminally Defiant Teen

← 1   2   3   4   5   6   7   8   9   10 →

Normal Teen Behavior: ADS 1-3
Nearly all teens are defiant at times. It's part of their quest to discover their own identity and attain a sense of independence. Challenging parental authority on occasion is part of the natural maturation process and should not cause great concern. Normal teen defiance may include occasionally raising their voice, occasional emotional disagreements, or the occasional expressions of stubbornness in an attempt to get their way.

Defiant Teen Behavior: ADS 3-5
Defiant teens participate in all the customary acts of normal teen defiance, and then some. What distinguishes defiant teens from those fur-

ther along the scale is that typical disciplinary actions will, in most cases, correct their behavior. When pushed, they will comply. These teens may break rules when given the opportunity, associate with other like-minded defiant teens, use illegal substances such as marijuana or alcohol, break school rules, sneak out of the house, regularly raise their voice at their parent and/or demonstrate a mindset of rebellion first, obedience second.

Extremely Defiant Teen Behavior: ADS 5–8

Extremely defiant teens demonstrate the same problem behaviors as defiant teens, and then some. The distinguishing characteristic of extremely defiant teens is that standard parental discipline choices do not seem to motivate a change in behavior. Their oppositional behavior is habitual and not easily contained. As noted child psychologist and author Douglas Riley puts it, the thoughts of this type of teen revolve "around defeating anyone's attempt to exercise authority over him."[1] The behavior of extremely defiant teens may include regular conflict with law enforcement, a continually agitated or angry attitude, threats of physical harm to those who resist their demands, and/or regular drug and alcohol use—all the classic characteristics of the juvenile delinquent.

Criminally Defiant Teen Behavior: ADS 8–10

These teens not only threaten violence, they *are* violent, and they do not comply with the wishes of any authority figure, including law enforcement. The behavior of these teens could be described as "out of control." They come and go as they please, challenging anyone to stop them from doing whatever they want to do, whenever they want to do it. Parents or school officials cannot manage the behavior of criminally defiant teens. Removal from the home or incarceration is the inevitable result of these teens' behavioral choices.[2]

Did you recognize your child's attitude and behavior on the scale? Did you see glimpses of your family's life, or did those negative behaviors seem alien to you? If your child rated below a 3 on the ADS scale, then congratulations on having a pretty normal teenager. This doesn't mean that your teen will not be a royal pain on occasion, but his or her behavior should not be considered out of the norm or a cause for concern. If you ranked your child higher than a 3, you may want to read on. The concepts and strategies in this book will specifically address the current issues in your family.

This adolescent defiance scale is a quick visual that underscores the fact that this book deals with issues most other Christian books on parenting do not. This doesn't mean, however, that the defiant behaviors outlined above are not present in many Christian homes. They are. Every day in my counseling practice, I meet with wonderful Christian parents who are battling with defiant kids. I consider this book a love letter to all those parents who feel as if they're alone in this struggle—parents whose families aren't perfect and who worry about what it means when they witness defiant behavior in one or more of their children. I want you to know that you are *not* alone and that there are proven methods to help you regain control in your home.

The Reality of Defiance

A set of exhausted, frustrated parents sat in my office describing the tension their 17-year-old daughter had created within their home. "She's extremely mouthy and disrespectful—doesn't listen to a word we say," the dad said. "She'll do whatever it takes to get her own way, and doesn't seem to care who gets hurt in the process."

"We've tried so hard to create a loving Christian home." Mom's words revealed her sadness. "Everyone at church used to say what a great family we have, but now . . ." her voice trailed off.

The scenes they described for me indicated a family on the verge of collapse. With all the yelling and fighting, it sounded like an episode of the *Jerry Springer Show*. These parents desperately wanted help in dealing with this out-of-control daughter, and they'd already tried a number of different approaches, all without success.

About halfway through our first session, the mother remarked, "One counselor we went to told us that the next time Kristi threw a fit about something, we were to just close our eyes and envision her as a three-year-old child throwing a temper tantrum. He said that's just what she is doing now, only she's older."

It wasn't the first time I'd heard such a comparison, but I wanted to offer these parents a more effective word picture for their teenage daughter's behavior.

"Actually," I said, "a better way to visualize the situation is to close your eyes and picture your daughter, not as an angry three-year-old, but rather as, oh, let's say, Osama bin Laden, turban and all." As loving parents, they were taken aback by the analogy, but as we talked it through, they came to recognize it as an accurate depiction of their daughter's behavior. Like many teenagers, she'd learned to employ a form of terrorist-like behavior to manipulate and control her parents.

Teens Who Act Like Terrorists

Like Kristi's parents, you may initially think that describing a teen's behavior as "terroristic" is rather harsh, but I've yet to find a more accurate picture for the defiant, out-of-control behavior I witness every day in many of the young people who walk into my counseling practice. Consider with me for a moment the manifesto of the terrorist: "Give in to my demands or you will pay a heavy price." Now consider the attitude of exceptionally defiant teens: "If you don't let me go out with the friends *I want*, go to the places *I want* and do the things *I want*, then I will make your life a living cesspool of misery and despair."

Of course, our kids seldom verbalize these threats explicitly (and I can't imagine one actually using the word "cesspool" in a sentence), but "do what I want or you'll be sorry" is unquestionably the intent of their attitudes and actions. And their parents, who aren't equipped to deal with such tactics, suddenly find themselves taken hostage to their child's defiant behavior.

Law enforcement officials in the United States follow one unwavering principle when it comes to kidnappings: *Never pay a ransom.* Is this approach insensitive or uncaring? Does it demonstrate a lack of compassion for the victims? No. This principle arises out of a larger principle for dealing with people who seek power through intimidation: NEVER NEGOTIATE WITH TERRORISTS. Why? *Because doing so only breeds more terrorism.* If the terrorist gains any kind of payoff for his threats, it emboldens him to keep on threatening people to get what he wants.

For example, if a thug kidnaps a business executive from a multinational corporation and receives a two-million-dollar ransom for his efforts, what do you think he'll do next? Invest that capital in mutual funds and diversify his retirement portfolio? No, he'll start looking for his next wealthy, well-connected victim, and he'll repeat the action that has proven to be successful in lining his pockets with cold, hard cash.

The lesson here is that if we let terrorism, in any form, pay off for the terrorists, then we are literally training them to keep doing what they are doing. This technique is called "reinforcement." Have you ever seen a handler toss a fish to a performing seal at Sea World? Why do they do that? To get the seal to do what the trainer wants it to do. The seal knows that it will get a payoff whenever it performs the trick correctly. Through positive reinforcement—that fish snack—the handlers have trained the seal to keep doing what it's doing.

I realize, of course, that the teenager at your house is neither a cold-blooded terrorist nor a gluttonous sea mammal, but the principle of reinforcement still applies. When we give in to the demands of our defiant teen just to avoid an angry explosion, then we are actually encouraging the very behavior that we claim to loathe. We are *reinforcing* the caustic behavior by allowing it to pay off for the child, and as a result, we find ourselves living in a nearly constant state of siege.

Since none of us wants to be held hostage in our own homes, this book is all about how to stop negotiating with the pseudo-terrorist in your home and how to begin restoring peace to your household as you regain the authority that God ordained for you, as a parent, to have.

You Are Not Alone

Although it may not sound that way when I refer to these little darlings as acting like terrorists, working with adolescents is the joy of my life. I invested 20 years as a youth minister in the local church, and for the past several years I've served as director of a Christian counseling center that specializes in working with adolescents and their families. I have three grown kids of my own, so my experience with teenagers is not just occupational or academic. During a stretch of about 10 years, our home was occupied by at least one of them.

I have been in every conceivable life situation with hundreds and hundreds of teenagers over the years. I have prayed with them, played with them, preached to them, listened to them, sung with them, cried with them and—on more than one occasion—run from them.

I am inspired by their passion and awed by their eagerness to look at the world around them and ask, "Why not?" But my love for them doesn't blind me to the fact that in some children's zeal to achieve their identity and independence, they develop habits that lead to selfishness, rudeness and an entitlement mentality. They really do seem to believe the world revolves around them. As the adults in their lives, it's our job to open their eyes to the truth that life is too precious a gift to waste on self-centered living.

It's difficult to keep the big picture in sight when you're in the heat of battle with an exceptionally defiant teen. When you're fully consumed with the fight to restore sanity to your home, you may find it difficult to summon the hope that life will ever get better. I'm here to tell you that it most definitely can.

Most of the parents who come to me for help are struggling with behavioral problems in their teens; they're simply overwhelmed by their child's defiance, rebellion, out-of-control anger and other disruptive behaviors. As one of the "guys" on staff, I tend to work with a lot of young men who come into the center, so I get to spend nearly all day, every day, dealing one-on-one with surly teenage boys. But I feel like General Patton when he was asked about what he thought of war: "God help me, I love it so!"

An equally fulfilling aspect of my job is working with the parents of these kids. Many are angry, frustrated and driven to their wits' end by how their home life has deteriorated. Often they also are burdened with a sense of failure and guilt, convinced that they are the only Christian parents who have had to pick up their child at the police station because she was arrested for shoplifting, or to walk their son out of school because he was expelled for drug possession.

If you're exasperated by a child's defiance, I want you to know that you're not alone. Out-of-control teenage behavior seems to be systemic throughout American culture, and this includes the Christian community as well. The parents who come to our counseling center include preachers, Sunday school teachers, deacons, elders, ministers and people who are actively rooted in the ministries of their churches. These are not bad people, bad Christians or bad parents. They're people just like you and me who deeply love their children but simply don't know how to cope with their threatening, manipulative tactics. My job is to equip them—and you—with the strategies they need to regain the upper hand. Through years of working with parents and their teens, I know without a doubt that change is possible, even in the most difficult situations.

As a Christian counselor I have the joy of watching the Great Physician heal individuals and families at our office all the time, and He gives me the privilege of having a front-row seat as He does it. I can assure you with confidence that no matter how desperate your situation may seem, God is sovereign over your family and your defiant child as well. In other words, He's right there with you in the battle.

Furthermore, God has given us the instructions we need to carry out His will and achieve victory. We won't always like those instructions (just ask the rich young ruler—see Mark 10), but we can cling to the knowledge that they are intended for our good, for our protection.

In Ephesians 6, Paul instructs us to put on the full armor of God because we're living in a war zone. I believe that some of the biggest battles are being waged in homes with defiant children. The kids, however, are not the enemy, no matter how bad their behavior may be. As Paul advises us, we do not battle against flesh and blood, but "against the rulers, against the authorities, against the powers of this dark world and against the spiritual forces of evil in the heavenly realms" (Eph. 6:12).

Your child is not the enemy; *he or she is the target of the Enemy*. To protect your precious gift from God, you are called to sacrifice yourself for his or her betterment and to put your child's needs above your own. Doing so will cost you time. It may cost you personal advancement. It will definitely cost you money. And sometimes the cost will be your child's resentment as you take a hard stand against his or her desires. But as painful as it is to see that stone cold look of hatred and resentment in the eyes of the child you love, you can trust that the feelings are only temporary. Inside, that teenager is a precious, eternal being whose future is worth fighting for.

The Heart of the Problem

I think it's odd that we so often refer to one of the most famous stories in the Bible as the parable of the prodigal son when it's actually the story of the prodigal *sons*. Plural. We tend to get so caught up in the salacious story of the young rebel brother that we forget all about the older brother who stayed behind with his dad. Sometimes we even cut the story off just after the young son returns home and his father runs out to meet him. But when we do that, we miss out on a powerful insight.

Do you remember how the father welcomed his younger son? He threw a party and killed a fatted calf to celebrate the wayward son's homecoming. But instead of joining the festivities, the older brother threw his own party—a pity party of one. When his father came to personally invite him to join the fun, the older brother exploded: "Look! All these years I've been slaving for you and never disobeyed your orders" (Luke 15:29). From his point of view, he'd wasted his time working his fingers to the bone, doing everything his father required of him—his father had never thrown him a party or even given him a lousy goat to barbecue with his friends. This son had lived by the rules, doing what he was supposed to do, when he was supposed to do it. But in this scene it becomes clear that, despite his outward good-boy appearance, in his heart the older son was just as disconnected from his father as his rebellious brother had ever been.

Like the older brother, we parents often work off a list, too. Our mental checklist may include ensuring that our kids . . .

- earn reasonable grades
- graduate from high school
- avoid problems with alcohol and drugs
- don't ever call us from the police station

• are not sexually active
• attend church without too much of a hassle

We seem to believe that if we're able to place a checkmark by each item on our list, then we can lift our heads high, confident in our success as Christian parents. But Jesus taught us that life is not about keeping a list. Christianity is not a bunch of dos and don'ts; it's all about the heart. It's about our child's heart—and ours—beating in rhythm with the heart of our heavenly Father. Rather than being satisfied with our child's outward compliance to the rules, we need to strive for their heart. Our greatest hope must be that they will make decisions that please the Lord—not because they are forced to do so, but because it's their greatest desire. Living a life that is pleasing to God should be a genuine reflection of who they are, deep within.

However, even though we won't be satisfied with outward compliance to the rules, that's where we have to start. A child's long journey to the heart of God must begin with outward compliance to the boundaries established in the home. By regaining authority within your family and helping your child rein in his out-of-control behavior, you are clearing the path ahead so that the rest of his spiritual journey can be completed successfully.

Effective Principles for Any Parent

I was 15 years old in 1975, and it was a beautiful Friday in my hometown of Cisco, Texas. My father, who was physically disabled due to a heart condition, had instructed me to mow the lawn that week, but with my busy schedule and hectic social calendar, I kept putting off this hated task. Every time I had delayed my work, my dad seemed not to realize it or respond. I don't know what had gotten into him. I wasn't sure what had caused this sudden streak of good luck, but so far so good.

Which brings me back to that particular Friday afternoon. I was in the bathroom preparing for a hot night out on the town with what I believe was called a "foxy lady" in 1975, when my dad stuck his head in and asked the one question I had been dreading all week: "Jim, did you mow the lawn like I asked?"

Of course I knew that he already knew the answer to his question, but maybe I could eek out just one more evening without succumbing to the inevitable. "Well, Dad, *technically* no. But listen, I've got a big date tonight and I've got nothing going on tomorrow, so I promise I'll do it then . . . okay?"

Well, it wasn't okay.

"No, you have put this off all week. You will mow it *now*—and lower the blades like I told you to last time, so that it cuts lower. No arguing. Just do it!"

There was no use trying to talk him out of it, so I threw on some shorts, ran to the garage, whipped out the lawnmower and got the grass cut in record time! While showering off the sweat and grass clippings, I was quite proud of myself. I was only going to be about 30 minutes late to my date. Maybe this night wasn't going to be a bust after all.

That's when I heard the door open again and my dad ask, "Jim, did you lower the blades like I asked you to?" I couldn't believe my ears. I couldn't believe he was being such a jerk!

"No dad, but I'm really late! I'll cut the whole thing again in the morning, but right now, I've really got to go."

And in reply, my dear old dad says, "No, what you're going to do is go back outside, lower the blades and do what I asked you to do, the way I asked you to do it." So, I mowed the lawn again. I lowered the blades and slowly and methodically mowed the entire thing. But I took special care to ram the mower into each tree and to slam it into the side of the house on each pass.

About the second time I almost knocked the mailbox off its pole, I felt a hand on my shoulder. I was forcefully turned around. My dad, all 120 pounds of him, looked me in the eye and said, "You hit that box one more time, young man, and you and I are going to tangle." Keep in mind that my dad was disabled, skinny, short and frail, while I was a strapping high-school football player. I mean, what was he going to do to me? Throw his support hose at me?

But you know what my reaction was? I was struck with fear. All the blood drained from my head as I replied, "Yes, sir." And I carefully finished mowing the yard.

Why did I respond that way? He really couldn't have done anything physically to me, and Mom wouldn't let him kick me out of the house. So why did I react with almost instinctive submission? Because way back in my early childhood, it was ingrained in me to respect my father and mother. Not because of what they could do to me, but because of *who they were*. Before I even knew that I had the option to defy my parents, they were teaching me the power of respect. That lesson, taught to me as a small child by my parents, paid off for them that Friday night as their son learned a valuable lesson, and a girl—I've forgotten her name—missed out on a great date.

That story leads me to a final note before we get started: Although this book primarily addresses the issue of parenting defiant teenagers, you'll find the principles helpful no matter what age your child is right now. As someone once wisely noted, *you parent your teenagers when they are two*. When the values of respect and submission to authority are instilled in the psyches of small children, they bear fruit when those children grow into teenagers. The overall philosophy outlined in this book can be adapted for children of any age, starting with toddlers.

Also, while I'm writing from the perspective of a Christian who believes God is involved actively in the lives of our children, the principles in this book apply to parents of any faith, or none, who are seeking to wrest control from the grasp of an extremely defiant child. My most earnest desire, however, is that within these pages you will find the Truth—the Truth that will lead you to seek out a personal relationship with your heavenly Father. Each of us will find greater hope and wisdom when we allow ourselves to be embraced by and learn from the greatest Parent of all, one who is well versed in dealing with extremely defiant children—like you and me.

IT'S NEVER TOO LATE

You can't swing a stick in Austin, Texas, without hitting a barbecue joint. If you could see my waistline, you'd understand just how knowledgeable I am on this subject. So when a pastor friend of mine called and asked if we could meet for lunch, I suggested Rudy's before he could come up with his own healthier suggestion.

After we had finished off our ribs (no sauce, just straight up) and started in on the banana pudding, he explained why he had wanted to talk with me: "I've finally decided to let Matt quit school and move out of the house. It's what he wants, and I'm tired of fighting." Seventeen-year-old Matt had been causing problems for years. He constantly made trouble at school and created heartache at home. This child had always been a source of pain and embarrassment for the family, so to my friend, letting him leave the house seemed like the best course of action for everyone involved. I'll never forget it how he explained his decision to me: "It's too late for my oldest boy. I've got to focus more on my younger ones."

At first I thought I'd simply misunderstood, but I soon realized I'd heard all too accurately. Here was a man of God, someone with more degrees than a thermometer, who every week offered words of hope and encouragement to hundreds of parishioners. Yet he was telling me that he'd given up all hope for his oldest child. He was prepared to write off this teenager as just one more casualty of the culture war and try to salvage what he could from the rest of his beleaguered family.

It's Never Too Late When God Is Involved

Despite my shock, I understood exactly where he was coming from. On a daily basis, I see that same look of despair and hopelessness on the faces of parents worn out by their exceptionally defiant teens. Some have fought the battle for so long that every reserve of hope has been drained. Like my pastor friend, they feel it's absolutely useless to fight any longer.

But feelings are not facts, which is why emotions are a terrible thing on which to base our life decisions. Remember: Just because you feel a certain way doesn't make it true. As Jeremiah 17:9 tells us, "The heart is deceitful above all things, and it is exceedingly corrupt: who can know it?" (ASV). But where our feelings fail us, the Word of God remains rock solid, and the resounding message throughout the Bible is that it's never too late for hope and healing when God is involved.

Let's look at just a handful of examples that illustrate this point. First, consider the story of Abraham, who waited decades for the child God promised, only to then be instructed to sacrifice his son. God didn't explain why; He simply ordered Abraham to go and kill Isaac. What's even more shocking is that Abraham agreed to do it! He had such faith that he obeyed without questioning, trusting that God had some greater purpose in mind.

So Abraham traveled with his son to the place of God's choosing. He put together the altar and prepared the fire and the wood, all the while hoping that the Lord would rescind the order and spare the life of his child. But no reprieve came. Just imagine how you would feel if your little boy looked up into your face and said, "Dad, here's the fire and the wood, but where is the lamb for the burnt sacrifice?" (See Gen. 22:7.) Abraham answered, "God will give us the lamb to sacrifice, buddy. Don't you worry about it." In an extraordinary act of faith, Abraham laid Isaac out on the altar. *At the very last instant,* just as he was in the act of raising the knife, the angel of the Lord cried out for him to stop. Abraham looked over his shoulder and saw a ram caught in a thicket, God's provision for the sacrifice. When all hope seemed lost, God came through.

Next, let's look at the story of Jesus' good friend Lazarus. When Lazarus became extremely ill, his sisters, Mary and Martha, sent word to Jesus, asking Him to come to their aid. They knew that Jesus could heal their brother, so they waited eagerly for His arrival. And they waited. And waited. But Jesus never showed up. At some point, Mary and Martha must have wondered exactly what was keeping their "good friend" Jesus. Just what was so all-fired important that He couldn't break away to help them?

Eventually, Lazarus, with his sisters by his side, succumbed to his illness and died. Still no Jesus. There was nothing left to do but bury their brother in the family tomb. Clearly, Mary and Martha no longer had reason to hope. When Jesus finally arrived four days after the funeral, Mary didn't even make the effort to go out and greet Him. But her despair was turned to joy when Jesus called into the tomb and Lazarus emerged very much alive. *When all hope seemed lost*, Jesus' presence changed everything.

Although the Bible is filled with last-minute saves like this, we'll look at just one more: the story of a woman whose life appeared to be one long series of broken promises and broken relationships. It's possible that she believed the only way she could gain the affection she craved was to give herself away sexually. She knew it was wrong, but it was likely the only life she had ever known. In fact, she emerges into the biblical narrative right in the middle of one such illicit tryst, when she's dragged from an adulterous encounter by a mob of angry religious leaders bent on vengeance and condemnation. She must have known the consequences specified in the Law for behavior like hers, but her blood must have run cold at the sight of all these angry men ready to take out their self-righteous anger on her. Hope must have abandoned her, along with every shred of dignity, as she was thrown to the ground and surrounded by men with their stones at the ready. She must have prayed that God, if He was real, would show more mercy to her in the next life than she had experienced in this one. She closed her eyes and waited for the inevitable.

But the inevitable never came. As she cowered on the ground, she heard a new voice, a Man who spoke to those religious leaders with a quiet authority. He seemed to be coming to her defense . . . and it was working! One by one, the men dropped their stones and walked away. As the realization dawned on her that they were not going to kill her after all, this extraordinary Man reached down and helped her to her feet.

Not only did He save her from a certain death, but He also told her of a way that she could be saved from her desperate life. Just when all hope seemed gone, this Jesus gave her a new life . . . in more ways than one.

In each of these encounters and countless more, *at the very last instant, when all hope seemed lost, the inevitable never came.* God changed everything. This is the kind of God we serve. He has made it His trademark to give hope to the hopeless and infuse life into certain death. This is what our God does, and faith means believing in Him despite our circumstances and regardless of our feelings.

If you are the parent of a defiant child, please know this: God's grace and redemptive power are far greater than any rebellion your child could ever throw at you. It is never too late for the God of second chances to supernaturally intervene in your home to bring about hope and healing.

Your Teen Is Still a Work in Progress

It has been said that teenagers are like cement, and they are setting fast. But the important thing to remember is that they are *still* setting. Just because your 14-year-old is emotionally out of control right now does not mean that he's always going to be that way. He still has a vast amount of learning, growing and experiencing to do, and as his parent, you hold the greatest potential to significantly influence all of that. Some parents understandably feel that it's too late to make any constructive changes in their teen's extremely defiant behavior, but Scripture and life experience tell us that this cannot be true.

Take me for example. I was a leader in my eighth-grade class. Before you get too impressed, you should know that I wasn't the leader of the student council or the leader in grade-point-average. No, I led the eighth grade in the number of licks I received from various teachers throughout the year. In the years before corporal punishment fell out of favor in public schools, the race to receive the most spankings always resulted in a heated competition at Cisco Junior High. That year, I nudged out Richard Cunningham the last week of school to secure the title. I received 64 licks that year, mostly from Mrs. Hart. (We'll discuss her class again a little later.) Unfortunately for me, the rule at my house was that for every spanking I earned at school, I received double the amount of licks when I got home. I walk with a slight limp to this day, while my parents developed exceptionally well-muscled forearms.

Now if someone had looked at my school file back then, based on all those episodes of corporal punishment they easily might have concluded that I was the next Charles Manson in waiting. However, my parents realized that I wasn't a bad kid—I was just a little feisty. They never said, "Sixty-four licks!? This boy is already a full-blown juvenile delinquent at age 13! Let's ship him off to military school, because he's beyond all hope." Instead, they just kept loving me, guiding me and correcting me through what I like to call my "rambunctious period."

Although I was certainly a handful, my behavior paled in comparison to that of Luke, one of the most defiant kids ever to drag his feet into my office. Among other things, he had been expelled for bringing weapons to school, had been caught using drugs, had been arrested for stealing and had driven his parents to desperation with his violent outbursts at home. His mom told me that the sight of police cars in front of their home had become such a common occurrence that their neighbors didn't even inquire about it anymore.

Even though Luke did fine in our one-on-one sessions, every time his parents joined us he became like a crazed animal, unable to control his anger and disdain for his parents. Their relationship finally became so unbearable that his parents had him removed from the home and placed in a residential treatment program. I honestly thought that he would attempt to burn the place down by the end of the first week, but I was wrong. In an environment where the rules were strictly enforced and expectations were made clear, he began to change. By the end of the first semester, Luke was giving campus tours, and soon after that he moved back home. We worked together for another year or so, and now he's in college, with a great GPA, looking ahead to law school.

By no means is Luke now a perfect young man, nor did he make these changes overnight. However, the transformation in him has been remarkable and demonstrates that every child is capable of changing significantly over time. His story affirms the fact that an adolescent is still a work in progress and may yet mature into a fully developed, healthy adult. This truth should give every parent reason for hope.

Escape the Cycle of Guilt

Many parents find themselves buried in despair, convinced that their poor parenting decisions in the past are the reason for their child's obnoxious behavior in the present. Every time there is an outburst at home or they get a call from the school principal about a behavioral issue, they're consumed with guilt, certain that they bear the blame for the problems their child is creating.

Parents who buy into this line of thinking often find themselves trapped in a cycle of feeding their child's oppositional behavior. For example, when Paula told 16-year-old Heather that she could not attend a party where no parents would be present, her daughter immediately started arguing and calling her names. Paula held her ground for over an hour, but when her daughter started yelling so loud that the next-door neighbors could hear, she finally snapped. Paula screamed at Heather, using language that she immediately regretted. Guilt instantly kicked into high gear. How could she be upset with her daughter when she, as the mom, was acting the very same way? Paula felt so bad about losing her temper that she decided to let Heather go to the party as a way of making it up to her.

Guilt works against us in insidious ways, and some kids know just how to use it against their parents. Twelve-year-old Ken has become an expert in the technique of terrorizing his dad, Ross, with guilt. During his own childhood, Ross hated that his old man missed all his football games and never even thought about taking him fishing or camping. He swore that he would never repeat that mistake when he became a father, but with his demanding job, it's not easy to spend as much time with the kids as he'd like.

Last week, Ross shared with me that he and his son visited an electronics store, and Ken demanded that his dad buy him the latest video game, the one with the "mature audiences only" warning label. Ross, to his credit, held his ground for a while. Then Ken pulled out his tried-

and-true trump card: "If you were home more, maybe I wouldn't have to just sit around and play video games all the time! You work so much, it's like I don't even have a dad! You're the worst father on the planet!" Racked with guilt, Ross gave in to the demands of his teenage terrorist and paid for the game without saying another word.

Guilt over past "bad" parenting decisions undermines our ability to make correct decisions in the present. Guilt is a tool of the Adversary that eats away at our souls and destroys our relationship with our kids. Does a parent's behavior influence the child? Absolutely. And do parents make mistakes? I've yet to meet one who hasn't. But rather than wallowing in guilt, we can let our recognition of past parenting mistakes motivate us to make positive changes and to look to God as our ultimate source of help.

Bad Combinations

Even as we commit ourselves to pursuing a healthier approach to parenting, we need to recognize that our children are independent moral agents who must accept responsibility for their own actions.

Do you remember the Los Angeles riots back in the early 1990s? As I watched those tragic events unfold on the TV, I heard one news correspondent state, "It was estimated that up to 50,000 people participated in the riots, with over 12,000 arrested. This proves that the looting, beatings and rioting are not being carried out by just thugs, gang members and criminals, but by the entire community. The entire population of South Central LA is reacting to the horrible levels of poverty, racism, lack of opportunity and unemployment." What he was saying made sense to me; in fact, I could see the truth of it for myself by just watching the TV.

Then another commentator made a strategically important point: "Wait a minute. More than a half a million people live in South Central Los Angeles, and just 50,000 may be participating in the riots? That's only 10 percent of the community. What about the other 90 percent? They have suffered through the same poverty, the same blatant racism, the same lack of opportunity and the same debilitating levels of unemployment, yet they are choosing not to participate in these criminal activities and to obey the law. Ninety percent are choosing to do the right thing."

So while environment certainly can lend insight into someone's behavior, it never *dictates* that person's behavior. Have our past parenting choices influenced our children's behavior? Yes. Do those past actions dictate our children's choices today? No. If all bad parenting choices dictated the behavior of children, then all children whose parents have made bad parenting choices would be extremely rebellious. And we know that this is just not the case.

So why is it that within one family, with the same set of parents, parenting the same way with all their kids, we often find such diversity in the behavior of those kids? We've all seen families like this: two of the children are very well behaved but the third revels in disobedience. Why is that?

Noted family expert Eduardo Bustamante, who has written extensively about disruptive teens, addressed the concept of "goodness of fit" when it comes to the emergence of defiant children within a family. [1] As we know, all children are born with individual temperaments. Some are naturally compliant, while others tend to be more defiant by nature. And parents likewise tend to have natural parenting styles. Let's look briefly at three of the more common approaches to parenting:

- **Lenient parents** choose the path of least resistance. Their driving motivation is to avoid conflict. They tend to want to be friends with their children, rather than authority figures.

- **Authoritarian parents** tend to be dictatorial. They emphasize parental control over relationship.

- **Authoritative parents** are primarily concerned with the relationship and the ultimate benefit of the child. They tend to establish clear boundaries, enforce those boundaries fairly and consistently, and place a high priority on unconditional love and acceptance.

Children respond to these parenting styles in different ways, depending on their own temperament. When a child who is naturally compliant interacts with a parent who tends to be naturally lenient, there is less chance for oppositional behavior to occur. On the other hand, if a naturally defiant child is parented by someone with a naturally authoritative style, there may be small skirmishes here and there but nothing serious.

However, if you combine a naturally defiant child with parents who are either naturally lenient or authoritarian, you get a very different result. Do you remember putting baking soda and vinegar in those little plastic rockets when you were a kid and watching them explode off the launch pad and shoot high into the air? That's a great picture of what you get with these parent-child combinations. Things can quickly build to explosive levels.

Such a situation lacks what Bustamante described as "goodness of fit." There is nothing fundamentally wrong with the child or the parent, but the combination naturally leads to disruptive behavior.

If you recognize yourself as one-half a bad combination, what can you do? Are you doomed to live in this house of conflict forever? If the challenges your family experiences are a result of your parent-child temperament combination, what hope do you have for change? The answer is *you*. *You* can deliberately change your parenting style in order to regain control in your home. *You* are the adult, and *you* are more spiritually mature, so *you* are the one who can take the initiative to change the relational dynamic in your family.

And if you don't believe that you can do this, that you are not up to the task, then you need to grab hold of one of the greatest promises that God gives us in the New Testament. Listen up, struggling parent, because these words from Paul are just for you: "I can do all things through Christ who gives me strength" (Phil. 4:13). It doesn't matter what challenge is before you, God's power will flow through you to accomplish that task. You can take it to the bank, because it's a promise from your God. Remember: It's never too late for your child to begin doing the right thing, and it's never too late for you, as a parent, to begin doing the right thing either.

HAVE A SEAT ON THE COUCH

1. What do the examples of hope from the Bible mean to you? Do they encourage you, or are they just tired old stories? Why?

2. Do you believe that the guilt brought about by past parenting mistakes has led you to make poor parenting decisions in the present? Why or why not?

3. Which style of parenting discussed in this chapter do you feel you adhere closest to? How does this style "fit" with the natural temperament of your defiant child?

4. Are there times when you feel as though your situation is beyond hope? When was the last time you felt that way?

5. What do you think Matthew 6:33 has to say to a parent who may be struggling with a defiant child in their home? Is this verse pertinent to our discussion? Why or why not?

SO WHEN DO WE START TO WORRY?

One of the biggest questions parents face is whether their child's behavior is just a normal part of testing the limits and growing into an independent person or is an indication that something serious is going on. A brief look at two teenagers may help us answer that question.

Jake

Jake just turned 15. He's failing most of his classes and hates anyone at school who is remotely popular. His wardrobe is restricted to black T-shirts that are too small, paired with dark girl's jeans. He has only a few friends, similarly dressed kids who share his interests . . . or lack thereof. Cannibal Corpse is his favorite band. If he could be bothered to talk with an adult, he would tell you that his room, decorated with his own artwork graphically depicting death and violence, is his private den where he can escape "the wretchedness of school, this sick self-righteous society and my messed up family." There, he can download his music, text his friends and smoke his weed—careful to blow the smoke out his window, of course.

"All I want is to be left alone. Is that too much to ask? Why can't my parents just leave me the @#$% alone?! They are constantly up in my face, telling me what to do, trying to control my life." Jake pauses, then talks more quietly but with a disturbing intensity. "They may think they control me, but as usual, they don't have a clue. I just ignore or work around their stupid rules. They can make me go to school, but I don't have to do the work . . . or even go to class. I may have to live in this house, but I don't have to hang out with my so-called family."

Jake has three more years "to live in this prison they call a home," and then he plans to get as far away from his parents as he can. In the meantime, if they don't respond to his demand that they "back off and leave me alone," then they are in for a long three years. He can guarantee them that.

For their part, Jake's parents don't know what to do. Although he has been a strong-willed child who resisted their efforts at discipline since toddlerhood, they had always been able to bring him around to reluctant obedience eventually. But recently his behavior has become all but uncontrollable.

The first time Jake blatantly defied his mother's authority was three years ago, while his dad was away on business. When his mom told him to get in the car so they could go to church, Jake simply told her, "No." When she insisted, he responded, "You can't make me do it." Taken aback by his deliberate defiance, she realized he was right. She couldn't "make him." He might only be 12 years old, but he was nearly as big as she was, and a lot stronger.

Now at age 15, Jake's defiance has only increased, along with his parents' sense of helplessness. They've tried every form of punishment they can think of, but nothing works. He just seems to laugh it off and keep doing what he wants. They hate to admit it, but they're afraid of their own son. "Well, maybe not afraid," his dad clarifies, "but we do feel intimidated by his threats and callous disregard for our authority—or any authority, for that matter."

His parents know that Jake can't wait for his eighteenth birthday so he can escape the house. And although they feel guilty about it, they are secretly just as eager to see him go.

Sam

Now let's consider Samantha—"Sam" to her friends and family. This 13-year-old earns solid grades, hangs out on the fringes of A-list popularity at school, and plays on the "B" team in volleyball. Sam is close friends with many of her teammates, and she's active in her youth group at church.

Although Sam and her parents used to have a good relationship, lately she has been getting more and more upset with them. She used to comply readily with their requests, but now she's starting to question their expectations and resist their guidance. "I used to think they were fair," she explains, "but now it seems like they're just making up rules as they go along. Their stupid reasons make no sense." When Sam was little, she would never have dreamed of telling her parents no if they asked her to do something, but now she feels almost as if it's her duty to put up some kind of resistance. "I mean, it's not like I'm their slave or anything," she notes. "Who gave them the right to tell me what to do?"

For their part, Sam's parents are rather upset too, although *bewildered* more accurately describes their feelings about this seemingly sudden turn in their daughter's behavior. "She's always been such a good girl," her dad says, "but now she seems to be morphing into someone I hardly recognize."

Her mom confesses that they've always dreaded the teen years. All they had ever seen or read about adolescence convinced them that those years would be full of inevitable turmoil and strife. Now their worst fears about Sam's teen years are coming true. She's a rebel without a clue.

But as they talk things through, these parents conclude that all in all, Sam's still a pretty good kid. Yes, she's trying their patience and she seems to be experimenting with some rebellion, but when it comes down to it, she complies after being disciplined. After a blowup, when things have cooled down, they can go up to her room, talk to her, hug her and mend any feelings that may have been hurt. "Sure, she's a little argumentative at times," Dad says, "but what teenager isn't?" When they see her out with her friends at church or talking with adults at school, interacting on her own, they feel a sense of pride in their little girl. "Yep, in spite of it all, I think Sam is going to turn out just fine," her dad concludes.

A Good Place to Start Is at the Beginning

Although Jake and Sam are both rebellious in their own way, both do not qualify as a seriously oppositional/defiant teen. Like Sam, almost all teens flex their "independence" muscles on occasion. Even though we parents may not like it, this behavior is normal. But when it escalates into aggressive defiance, we need to pay attention, and the clues that a child may be heading into this dangerous zone often come long before the teen years.

Remember the early years of your child's life, when you watched in awe the almost daily evolution of her growing abilities? It is utterly fascinating to witness the psychological, physiological, emotional, cognitive and spiritual development of a young child. What joy it brought us parents to watch our little ones struggle with and master each developmental stage. We feel so proud to see our offspring advancing through the maturing process, acquiring new skills and a greater understanding of their world.

If I was a betting man—and as an ordained Southern Baptist minister I can assure you I am not . . . very often . . . or for very much—I would wager that you have a video of your child's first steps or her first word. It's natural to treasure the memories of such significant milestones. Yet those early achievements highlight a bittersweet moment: That first step you celebrated so enthusiastically signaled not only your child's physical growth but also her first step away from Mom and Dad. A child's increasing maturity inevitably brings increasing independence of thought and action.

Once, when my daughter Sarah was two years old, I cautioned her not to touch the nice flower vase on the coffee table. In response, my little darling slowly lifted her right hand and—looking me straight in the eye—smeared her grimy little finger all over that vase. I couldn't believe it! This was the first time that she had ever openly defied me. Immediately my father's heart plummeted with the fear that I had sired a wanton criminal. My mind filled with visions of the future: my daughter dropping out of school, falling into drug use and becoming pregnant at 16. Such are the naïve fears of young parents. However, these demonstrations of autonomous, self-determining thought and action are normal, expected and healthy for any properly developing child.

So when does this normal developmental behavior morph into rebellion that warrants inviting a British nanny and her reality-show camera crew to follow your family around for a week? Certain early childhood behaviors should get our attention if they continue over a significant period of time. These include but are not limited to:

- Breaking things in a rage
- Flagrant disregard of parental instructions
- The old standard: Doesn't work or play well with others
- Obsession with retaliating when wronged
- Habitual dishonesty to avoid consequences
- Relentlessly combating normal family routines, such as bedtime

Of course, various experts offer differing measures for deciding if a child has significant behavioral problems. For example, Russell Barkley and Christine Benton, in their book *Your Defiant Child,* state that they look for three things when assessing oppositional/defiant behavior in children. First, the child does not start doing what he was asked to do within one minute. Second, the child does not finish tasks that you ask him to do. And lastly, the child violates rules of conduct already established in the family.[1]

No matter what list is followed, everyone agrees that at some point developmentally appropriate behavior becomes inappropriate. Again, keep in mind that all children act out in these ways from time to time. The trigger for concern is if a young child demonstrates many of these attributes excessively, over at least a six-month period of time.

The answer to "why" this slippery slide from normal to abnormal occurs is a much more interesting discussion. Most people in the field of child psychology will tell you that aberrant early childhood behaviors stem from either the child's genetically predisposed brain physiology or the family structures the child is born into—or a combination of the two.

W. G. Ross, in his book *The Explosive Child*, describes his belief that just as some kids lag behind in reading or athletic skills, so some kids lag behind in the social skills of flexibility and frustration tolerance. Oppositional/defiant children do not choose to be explosive anymore than another child would choose to have a reading disability. They just need extra time and attention to attain these vital social skills. He believes that ample research suggests that physiologically based developmental delay is the root of most defiant childhood behavior.[2] As mentioned at the beginning of the book it, is also wise not to rule out the possibility of other psychological disorders, such as Attention Deficit Hyper Activity Disorder (ADHD), and their negative impact on the behavior of a child.

Other experts find that triggers in the home environment of these children serve as the primary cause for anger and impulsive behavior. For example, Robert Shaw, in his book *The Epidemic: The Rot of American Culture, Absentee and Permissive Parenting, and the Resultant Plague of Joyless, Selfish Children* (that may be the greatest book title ever!), recounts reading a parenting magazine that featured a Q&A section. One reader wrote to ask about her three-year-old who, though an otherwise wonderful child, pitched a fit whenever she was told "no." This little girl would throw herself on the floor, yelling that her mommy was not her mommy anymore.

The mother wanted to know if this sort of behavior should be considered normal. Dr. Shaw was dumbfounded to read the answer from the noted pediatrician, who declared that this sort of behavior was perfectly normal for a three-year-old. I echo the exasperation of Dr. Shaw's response to the advice columnist: "If this were normal, why would anyone want to have a child? Children are being injured in their emotional development every day by being allowed to behave in totally inappropriate ways."[3]

In addition to inept parenting advice from so-called "experts," numerous environmental conditions can injure the emotional development of young children. Some are fairly obvious:

- Divorce, particularly if ex-spouses are warring
- Frequent angry outbursts in the home by parents or siblings
- Violence witnessed or experienced by the child in the home
- Open drug and alcohol use in the home
- A discipline structure that is vague, lacks boundaries and is erratically enforced
- Absent, neglectful or self-consumed parents

This list is far from complete, but the bottom line is that numerous environmental factors can negatively influence a child's ability to develop appropriate anger-management and conflict-resolution skills.

So which came first, the chicken of genetics or the egg of environment? Is the behavioral culprit Nature or Nurture? My personal opinion is that the later the onset of the aberrant behavior, the better the odds that the child's environment has played a vital role. Conversely, the earlier a child shows extreme defiance, the greater the chance of a physiological root. For example, Ryan's mother sat weeping in my office as she described how her son had fought them from birth. Even as an infant, when his mother or father tried to cuddle or caress him, he would cry and push their faces away with his tiny little hands. Ryan came out of the womb angry, and that intense emotion never abated. Now, if Ryan's mom is telling the truth—and I have no reason to doubt her—this boy's defiant behavior started long before his parents had time to mess up his psyche. In my opinion, there can be little doubt of a strong physiological component to Ryan's battle with anger and impulse control.

By contrast, most of the parents who visit my practice did not observe extremely defiant behaviors until their child entered middle school. I often hear comments such as, "My daughter has always been such a good kid" and "Our son has never given us any trouble before now." This sudden, unexpected change in an early adolescent's behavior can, many times, be traced back to certain environmental issues within the home.

Consider a child who has been relatively compliant most of her young life. At the ripe old age of 12, when just the right synapse connects in her growing brain, she is struck with the sudden realization that she does not "have" to do what her parents say. You see, the onset of puberty marks a vital stage of cognitive and emotional development. As a child's brain begins the transformation into an adult brain, she enters a new phase of life that, much like toddlerhood, is epitomized by the need to exert her independence.

In fact, at this age, pleasing and being accepted by their peer group now trumps the approval and acceptance of their parents. Many parents report seeing the first signs of extreme rebellion during the late child-hood or early teen years. Apparently the "tweens" can be just as terrible as the "twos." Couple this with certain family environment elements, and it's not surprising that open defiance soon follows.

Another clue I look for is how widespread the oppositional behavior is. Does the child yell and scream at teachers, coaches and school admin-istrators? Is he constantly in trouble at school for disruptive and disre-spectful behavior? Or does he only act this way at home? Are the parents and siblings the only objects of the defiant child's wrath? I find that if the child reacts defiantly in all situations—home, school, church—then we may be dealing with a problem that is more serious and possibly physiological. But if the child only acts defiant and disrespectful at home, then that suggests that the home environment has taught him that he *can* behave in this negative manner and, at least from his point of view, get away with it.

What Should Be Considered Typical Teen Behavior?

In the United States, "adolescence" is an ambiguous term, encompass-ing a broad period between childhood and adulthood. Did you know the term "teenager" was not even in the American vernacular before 1941? That's because prior to the early twentieth century, a person was either a child or an adult. There was no confusing middle ground back when American culture revolved around a more rural lifestyle. Children went to school for a few years while they worked the land along side their parents. Then, at a relatively young age, they were considered adults, with all the related responsibilities. They were expected to earn their own living, get married and start having children of their own. In the good ol' days you didn't need to go off and "find yourself." You were easy to find: You were the 18-year-old in the field picking cotton 14 hours a day in order to feed your wife and small child. Your identity as a farmer was set, and you were independent from your parents, whether you wanted to be or not.

Enter the tectonic shift in the early 1900s, as many of these rural farming families migrated to the cities for better work and more pay.

Later, the Great Depression, child labor laws and the fact that secondary education was all but unheard of for the average American, colluded to create a large group of no-longer-children-but-not-yet-adults with a lot of time on their hands. In the late '30s, education started extending into the later teen years. By the 1950s, these not-yet-adults were cruising the drag, going to drive-in movies and wearing poodle skirts. Thus, "teen culture" was born. Then came the mass confusion of the '60s and '70s, the gluttony of the '80s and '90s, and now, after the dawning of a new century, we have a culturally entrenched subgroup of 12- to 22-year-olds who have no idea who they are or what life is about.

Have you ever seen a movie where a person starts out looking normal and then through computer-generated special effects, his face morphs into another creature? Well, you know when that transformation is in that "in between" stage—the stage when the person is not really a human or another creature but an unrecognizable *thing*? In human development terms, that's adolescence. Adolescents are no longer children, but they are not yet adults. They are unrecognizable *things* we call "teenagers." They enter the teen years as a child; go through a tumultuous emotional, psychological, spiritual and physical transitional phase; and, theoretically, emerge on the other side as well-balanced, fully functioning adults. The teen years afford your child the opportunity to figure out who she is and what her purpose is. Her job, during the teen years, is to seek out independence and discover her own identity. And that identity will increasingly have less to do with you and more to do with the outside world—namely, her peers.

When your daughter comes downstairs for church and you comment on how pretty she looks, you know she's started adolescence if she rolls her eyes, turns around and goes back to change her clothes. This is a clear indication that she is seeking independence from her parents and wants to create her own identity.

For teenagers, peer opinion often trumps parental opinion. During this period, a child's sense of self-worth is being solidified. Robert McGee, in his wonderful book *Search for Significance,* suggested a formula by which many people determine their self-worth:

Performance + Other People's Opinion = Our Self-worth[4]

McGee makes it clear that as believers we *should* base our self-worth not on the view of others but on who we are in Christ.[5] However, his formula accurately describes how most teenagers view themselves. During the teen years, a child begins developing the skill of personal reflection and insight. They consider their performance in areas such as academics, athletics or relationships with peers and evaluate how they stack up against others. Couple this with their perception, accurate or not, of how their peers are judging their performance, and you have an adolescent twisted in knots by the competing motivations to fit in while also standing out.

This drive to shape an independent identity can yield some positive results. Have you ever wondered why so many kids make meaningful spiritual decisions during their teen years? One reason is that, as a child, their faith was closely tied to the faith of their parents, pastor or Sunday school teacher. They believed because these significant people believed. But during their teen years, they recognize a need to believe in Christ because that is who *they* are. *They* are seeking to make Christ a part of *their* identity and to commit to that relationship *independently* from their parents and others.

However, this search for independence and identity also propels a teenager into conflict with parents. They want to dress differently than their parents, listen to different music than their parents and take different social or political views than their parents. This is not something to be alarmed about. These steps toward independence should be celebrated just as much as those first physical steps or first words, because they indicate that a child is growing up in a healthy, productive manner.

So some conflict is normal, and most teens fall into the normal defiance category. At my speaking engagements around the country, I always ask the parents in the crowd how many of them were very rebellious as teenagers. Usually, only about 10 percent of the hands go up— and this number remains consistent no matter where I'm speaking or to what kind of a parent group. The fact is, no matter what you've read about raising teens, very few are hardcore defiant delinquents. If your teen is ornery at times and talks back on occasion, take heart and know that he is in the midst of an age-appropriate search for his individual identity, well on his way to independence and developmental success.

However, if your child's defiant behavior extends beyond this and normal disciplinary methods don't seem to have any effect on him or her, then you may want to watch for some specific signals of what you're dealing with.

The Four Horsemen of the Teenage Apocalypse

Let's consider four characteristic behaviors that signal an adolescent is slipping outside the "normal" range of teenage angst. I call them the "four horsemen of the teenage apocalypse" because if your child demonstrates all four of these attributes, you're probably convinced that your world is coming to an end! Again, please keep in mind that nearly all adolescents exhibit these qualities *to some degree, at some times.* The teen who exhibits all or most of them to an extreme degree and as a general pattern of behavior over at least a six-month period can be considered an oppositional child. In those situations, you'll need the more serious, deliberate disciplinary tools we'll be discussing in later chapters.

Horseman 1: The Adolescent Narcissistic Fantasy

How well do you remember your eighth-grade Greek mythology? Does the name Narcissus sound familiar? This mythical character found himself so fascinating that he stared at his own reflection in a pool until he eventually fell in and died. His name now provides the root of the modern term "narcissist," which describes someone who is totally self-consumed, self-centered or self-absorbed.

This literary refresher course brings us to what I call the adolescent narcissistic fantasy. Yes, most teenagers lean toward the self-centered side. Empathy—the ability to relate to someone else's pain—is connected to a mature cognitive ability that many teens don't yet possess. As the late, great Keith Green sang, "It's so hard to see, when my eyes are on me."[6] Most teenagers keep their eyes firmly fixed on themselves, so it's difficult for them to see the perspectives of others. Kids enveloped in the adolescent narcissistic fantasy, however, go beyond the norm to exhibit narcissism on steroids. They are so consumed by this fantasy that they're convinced only they and their friends know what is true, right, just and good. Everybody else is an idiot.

In this child's fantasy world, he is always the victim, always right and never at fault, under any circumstances. Let me repeat that again: It's *never* his fault! If he's in trouble at school, it's because the teacher unjustly picks on him. If he's in trouble at home, it's because his parents are stupid and unfair. If he gets in trouble with the police, it's because the cops are out to get him and his friends.

What's striking about this type of teenager is that he will stick with this fantasy even when all evidence shows that he's being completely and utterly irrational. For example, 16-year-old Ben came into my office one day furious because a teacher was picking on him. She had accused him of throwing paper wads at another student in the class, and he was livid. He'd been in trouble with this teacher many times before, so he already had a reputation for being disruptive in her class. When she turned around from the blackboard, she saw Ben with paper wads on his desk. In addition, not only did the victim identify Ben as the wad thrower, but also when she asked the rest of the class who did it, they testified in unison that they saw Ben throw the paper wad. Seems fairly cut-and-dried, right? But from Ben's distorted viewpoint, because her back was turned and the teacher didn't *actually see* him throw the paper wad, she had no right to accuse him. He was consumed with righteous indignation at this totally unjust harassment.

A teen consumed by the adolescent narcissistic fantasy has no choice but to stick to a ridiculous point of view like this. If he ever allowed for even the possibility that he was in any way culpable for his misdeeds, then his whole fantasy world would come crumbling down. The narcissist *has to* always be right, always be innocent, always be misunderstood and always be persecuted. Giving just an inch and admitting to any possible responsibility for negative actions opens the floodgates of honesty and compels reexamination of all past behaviors. If he admits he is wrong in this current situation, then he may have to admit that he was wrong in other situations—and that his parents, teachers, principals or the police were actually right after all. Since that is just too ghastly a concept to even consider, Ben believes himself to be unquestionably justified in protesting his teacher's accusation. That's his story, and he's sticking to it.

Horseman 2: An Exaggerated Sense of Entitlement

Janet already felt exhausted as she started putting away her third load of laundry for the day. Every Saturday, she had to wade through a mountain of laundry before she could even start cleaning the house. But with three older kids and a husband who's convinced the church softball team would flounder without him, this was the reality of life for the moment.

Janet's train of thought derailed when she pulled open a dresser drawer to put Sean's socks away and noticed a small plastic bag peeking out from under the clothes. She took it out and then moved to the window to examine its contents under brighter light. As she opened the curtains and light filled the room, all the blood in her head drained away. Although she'd never actually seen marijuana before, she was confident that she was holding a baggie full of it. Her son was keeping illegal drugs in his drawer alongside the Simpson's boxers she'd bought him for Christmas! After all they had drilled into him about the danger of drug use, how could he do something like this?

Janet gathered herself and called her husband to come home. When he arrived, they discussed exactly how to handle this situation with Sean. They prepared exactly what each of them would say when they confronted their son: Janet would cover how disappointed they were in him, but that they still loved him and always would, while his dad would lay out clear consequences for this unthinkable breach of trust.

A few hours later, Sean came home from a friend's house, and his parents asked to see him in the den. When the 16-year-old entered the room and saw his baggie of pot sitting on the coffee table, neither of them got the opportunity to recite their prepared speeches because Sean erupted like Mount St. Helens. His face turned blood red, his eyes became wide and wild, and he shook his stash in his parents' faces while screaming, "You had no right! You had no right to go through my stuff! That is my drawer, with my things in it! And it's in my room, and you have no right to go in there and go through my things! I can't believe you! I'll never, *ever*, trust either of you again! *Ever*!!" He stormed out of the room, and when he slammed his door upstairs, all the family photos lining the hall shook with the vibration.

"This is my [fill in the blank]! You have no right!" How often have you heard those words before? It's called an exaggerated sense of entitlement. Some kids feel they are entitled to all the good things in life, without any of the resulting responsibilities. Sentiments like these have been echoed by countless teens in countless situations. Here are some all-time favorites:

- "This is *my* Facebook page! You have no right to look at it!"
- "This is *my* phone! You have no right to look at my text messages!"
- "This is *my* car! You have no right to go snooping around in it!"
- "This is *my* backpack! You have no right to go digging through it!"

Blind with fury that their parents have violated their personal space and messed with their personal belongings, they can't possibly see anything they may have done wrong themselves.

But let's look at the facts: In most states, a child under 18 years of age does not, for all practical purposes, own anything. I realize that this is getting down to nitty-gritty legalities, but it's true. A minor cannot own property in the way an adult might. They may have something held for them in trust, but an adult administers that ownership until they reach legal age. Technically, your daughter doesn't own her iPod, her Xbox or her cell phone. She doesn't own her jeans with the holes in them, the posters on her walls or the underwear in her drawers. She doesn't own anything, because legally, that's not the way it works. Even if she bought a car with her own money, the title would have to be in an adult's name. So the use of the word "my" is a relative term, because nothing in their world actually belongs to our teens.

So let's put to rest those emotional accusations that you are "violating my space"—along with any guilt you might feel for doing so. That space is *yours* and you have the right—and in some situations, the obligation—to know how it's being used. Don't get me wrong: I'm all for trusting your kids and allowing them a measure of privacy; but when they give you clear reason not to trust them, then all bets are off. A loving parent will look in every drawer, under every bed and in every shoebox to get between his or her child and destructive behaviors. So until your teenager can produce a check that he's written for rent on that room you are kind enough to let him occupy, it belongs to you. For most kids, this discussion of who-owns-what never comes up, but for an extremely defiant child, it is a concept that must be clearly understood.

But since most kids tend to reflect at least some slight sense of entitlement, when do you know if your child has an exaggerated one? We're back to the irrationality issue. Many kids have a hard time with gratitude. If you're waiting for your youngster to stop and write a note thanking you for all that you have done for them, you will be waiting a very long time. We may have reason for some unease, however, if a child never, ever expresses gratitude and empathy. If this grandiose, exaggerated sense of entitlement persists over several months and it appears with the other horsemen, then you may have cause for concern.

Horseman 3: Defiance Becomes a Persistent Pattern of Behavior

In my counseling practice, I deal with so many families who are completely exhausted. The parents come into my office with a look akin to battle fatigue. They wake up every morning only to begin another day of relentless conflict with their child.

We're not talking about teens who are just grumpy in the morning or react negatively to discipline; these defiant kids seem to *always* be in a bad mood and to *never* be willing to let hostilities die down. They wear their defiance like a suit at church. They don't mind making a scene at the mall. And whenever they are home, the conflict and tension are absolutely palpable. These families live in a never-ending cycle of rage, conflict and argument that continues day after day, week after week, month after month and year after year. In many cases, the incessant nature of the oppositional behavior slowly wears on the fabric of family relationships until almost no hope remains for peace and normalcy.

This persistent pattern of behavior rides in as the third horseman of the teenage apocalypse.

You probably know someone—or perhaps live with someone—for whom lying has become a habit. Habitual liars don't need a reason to be dishonest; they'll lie when no major consequences hang in the balance and even when there is no legitimate reason not to tell the truth. They lie about inconsequential things simply because that's their habit. They do it without thinking. In a similar way, some children fall into a type of "unthinking" oppositional behavior. They seem to rebel against parental authority out of principle, they argue for the sheer joy of arguing and they automatically vent hatred and discontent on nearly everyone around them. If this happens over a prolonged period, it's time to consider the possibility that your child is exceptionally defiant and outside the norms of teen behavior.

As noted earlier, all teens will ride with one or more of the four horsemen on occasion, and a persistent pattern of defiant behavior is no different. Yes, nearly all teens will be defiant at times, but those times are punctuated with periods of tranquility and relative compliance. *Most teens have reasons for being upset.* That statement may strike you as overly generous, but stay with me: Although a child's reasons may not make sense to us, most of them truly believe they have just cause for defying the authority of their parents. Perhaps you denied your son his beauty sleep by making him get up from a three-hour nap to help with the yard work. Or maybe you ruined your daughter's social life by forcing her to forego a trip to the mall with her friends so that she could join the family in celebrating Grandma's birthday at a cafeteria, followed by a game of dominoes at home. Whatever the circumstance, in the teens' estimation they have been grievously wronged, and it is their sacred duty to communicate that injury to you as the parent.

Individual instances like these may be aggravating, but it is the all-encompassing nature of prolonged acts of disobedience that signals a potential problem. When this becomes a constant state of bitterness and irritation disconnected from reason, your child's rebelliousness may be weaving itself into the very fabric of her personality, and thus cause for concern.

Horseman 4: "Normal" Methods of Discipline Don't Remedy the Problem

Jenny worked on her plan all week. Then, late Friday night, she put that plan into action. She stealthily made her way downstairs and disabled the alarm system. Then she went back upstairs, slipped out her bedroom window, climbed down the trellis and into a waiting car to join her boyfriend, Chad. Several hours later, she crawled drunkenly back into her bedroom only to find her parents sitting on the edge of her bed. And they weren't just waiting to tuck her in. The jig, as they say, was up.

The next day, after having time to reflect on the night's events, Jenny admitted her regret over sneaking out. She had ever done anything like this before, and given a one-month grounding, loss of her cell phone, loss of computer use, loss of her iPod and a ton of additional chores around the house, she would never do anything like that again. It just wasn't worth it.

That same weekend in a home nearby, Ashley used her own tried-and-true method of sneaking out. Her parents were sound sleepers, so she simply got dressed and walked out the back door. A car full of friends picked her up on their way to the party, someone handed her the first joint of the evening and away she went. Hours later, as she slipped in the back door just before dawn, she noticed the light on in the living room. Her parents asked her to take a seat and then explained that she would be grounded for breaking the house rules. Ashley just laughed. "You can't keep me here," she stated. "I can leave any time I want, and there's nothing you can do about it." As her parents raised their voices to object to her callous disregard of their parental authority, she flipped them the finger, staggered back to her room and slammed the door. Her parents stood their ground and Ashley remained on restriction for a week or so. Then she celebrated her return to the social fast lane by sneaking out with her friends the same night her grounding ended. There was a massive party on the other side of town, and she was not going to miss out.

Like Ashley's parents, many say, "We've tried everything! Nothing works!" Their children seem impervious to punishment. They've tried grounding them, confiscating treasured belongings, keeping them from events or people they desire, making them do unpleasant chores around the house—all to no avail. The kid either laughs it off, screams about their parental ineptitude or stoically endures the punishment only to continue the same behavior that got her into trouble in the first place. Do all teens resist or ignore discipline on occasion? Of course. But if your child's negative behavior is not restrained by "normal" parental discipline choices over a prolonged period of time, it's time to take a new approach.

To Sum It Up

Nearly all teens exhibit "rebellious" behaviors from time to time. Occasional conflict and friction with parents should be expected as teens seek to establish their own identities and independence. You don't need to freak out on the rare occasion that your 14-year-old daughter yells that she hates you for not letting her go to a party.

We should keep our eyes open for the four horsemen of the teenage apocalypse as signs that a child's behavior has crossed the line into a territory of concern. We want to be diligent in observing behavior over several months, watching for signs of the adolescent narcissistic fantasy, detecting symptoms of an exaggerated sense of entitlement, discerning whether their defiance is becoming a persistent pattern of behavior and noting if "normal" methods of discipline don't remedy the problem.

HAVE A SEAT ON THE COUCH

1. Did you see signs of defiant behavior in your child even when they were young? What behaviors specifically caused you concern?

2. Do you believe that there are environmental conditions that have contributed to your defiant child's behavior? What are they and how might they have been a factor?

3. Is your defiant teen defiant in places such as school, or is he only defiant at home? If he's only defiant at home, do you believe that a contributing factor is that in some way he is allowed to act that way at home? Why or why not?

4. Which of the four horsemen of the teenage apocalypse do you see most in your child? How do you see this demonstrated?

5. After reading this chapter, do you believe that your child's behavior is something to be concerned about, or is it just a natural expression of her desire for independence and to seek her own identity?

RULES WITHOUT A RELATIONSHIP

The defiant behavior of a teenager is seldom, if ever, about the "harshness" of the rules that have been established in the home. Of course, you'd never know this from the petulant complaints of some teens. See if any of these phrases ring a bell:

- "I can't believe you're such a Nazi!"
- "None of my friends' parents have stupid rules like this! Why can't you just be normal?"
- "This is so unfair!"

Just this week, a young man sat in my office sounding off about how "crazy" his parents were. He actually said, with a straight face, "All of my friends get to go out wherever they want, whenever they want, with anyone they want to. Why are my parents such idiots?!"

In my experience, plenty of families rigidly enforce some fairly strict rules with no regard for how their approach stacks up against that of other families in their community, and many of those family members just love all over each other. In other families, rules are practically unheard of. These are the homes of the "cool" parents who provide alcohol for all the youth and smoke weed with their kids. Their hazy reasoning goes something like this: "Like, God made like the herbs, dude, so it's, like, natural. How can you say that's, like, wrong . . . like?" And many of these anything-goes families fight like cats and dogs. So the presence of strict rules does not seem to be a determining factor in the level of peace and tranquility in the home, nor is there a clear connection between strict rules and overly rebellious children. So if the source of a teenager's anger and bitterness is not the severity of the rules in the home, to what can we attribute it?

In a word, *relationship*. Noted theologian Oscar Thompson, in his book *Concentric Circles of Concern,* identifies relationship as the most important word in the English language. Why? Because without it nothing else of importance could exist.[1] Without relationship, there can be no communication, love, art, community, service, music or sacrifice. So before we launch into specific parenting strategies for regaining control of a defiant teen, we must first examine what I believe to be the primary contributing factor of unruly behavior: a breach in the parent-child relationship.

Years ago, I heard teen expert Josh McDowell observe, "Rules without relationship equals rebellion." I appreciated that catchy and poignant statement, and during my years as a youth minister, I'm sure I used it many times in talking to my Wednesday night youth group. But it wasn't until I started my counseling career and sat in front of countless distraught families that I realized how many people are living representations of this statement. Almost without exception, if a family has trouble with an oppositional, defiant teenager, a broken relationship lies at the heart of the conflict.

Carla and her husband came into my office distraught over the increasing anger and bitterness of their 14-year-old daughter. They had no idea why she seemed to be mad at the world. As Carla related some examples of the nightmare that had become their family life, I couldn't help but notice her cutting wit and biting sarcasm. She mentioned making such comments to her daughter as, "Wake up and smell the coffee, little princess, because your mouth isn't going to save you from this one" and "Oh yeah, that's really a bright idea, Sherlock! If you had a brain, you'd probably take it out and play with it!"

As she continued describing her issues with her daughter in this condescending and demeaning tone, I finally interrupted to point out the offensive nature of her communication style. (We'll take a closer look at sarcasm in a later chapter.) Carla seemed surprised by my comments, but her husband meekly rolled his eyes in silent agreement. I explained that if she took that tone with me on a regular basis, I'd be angry and bitter too. Her passive-aggressive way of sarcastically cutting to the core of her child's self-esteem may not have caused the defiant behavior, but it certainly exacerbated the situation. At the core of this family conflict was a breach, primarily in the mother-daughter relationship, and it had to be repaired before any progress could be made in changing the child's behavior.

The Young and the Restless

This slow slide into a dysfunctional parent-child relationship tends to begin long before the behavioral problems become apparent. During a child's early years, parents establish or formulate several different types of relationships as part of the many-faceted dimensions of their daily interactions. In addition to the obvious guardian/dependent interactions, there is the teacher/student relationship, the coach/player relationship or even the warden/inmate relationship. In all the push and pull of these multiple roles, parents sometimes fail to establish a human, loving, intimate, *real* relationship with their kids.

Reflecting on your child's preadolescent years, does it seem as if you were *always* the watchful parent, *always* the instructive teacher, *always* the motivating coach or *always* the supervising warden? Did you ever remove the authoritarian mantle of the "adult commissioned to mold and guide" and just hang out with your young child, delighting in her as a person without engaging in any obligatory "life lessons"? Did you find occasions to laugh together, poke fun together, wonder about things together and enjoy one another's company?

Last night I was heading into Target, for about the tenth time this week, when I noticed a young mom's interaction with her son, who was maybe 10 years old. He would pretend he wasn't paying any attention, then quickly bump her rump with his and laugh hysterically. Instead of scolding him for engaging in improper, rough-housing behavior in a business establishment, this way-cool mother bided her time, then quick as a cat, bumped *his* rump with hers. Then, shaking with laughter, they walked on into the store together, her arm around his shoulder and his arm around her waist. If I could have been certain they wouldn't call store security, I would have run up to this lady and stuck a big gold star on her forehead. She gets it!

Sometimes I think that because we don't exactly know how to relate to children when they first arrive on the scene, we slip into one of these ready-made, well-defined parenting roles and play the part. In doing so, our relationship with our children can become detached and somewhat superficial. What's worse, our children sense that something is wrong. They start believing, perhaps unconsciously, that Mom isn't really genuine or that it doesn't feel like Dad actually cares about them. When a teenager cries out, "You don't even know me!" he is really saying, "You've never known me. You were just playing the part of the parent and I got stuck in the slot of your child. You were just 'the teacher' and I was stuck in the slot of student. My whole life, you've never treated me like a real person."

If we are to relate to our children the way God relates to us, then we have to start by establishing a genuine, honest relationship.

Developmental Change

While we're on the subject of younger children, let's talk about another topic that can lead to the deterioration of the parent-child relationship: developmental change. Now, I'm not referring to a child's normal developmental changes but to how we as parents need to developmentally change over time. Just as you cannot parent a 5-year-old as if she had the understanding of a 15-year-old, so you can't parent a 15-year-old as you would a kindergartner. When you take into account that the parenting process spans two decades and countless physical, psychological, emotional and spiritual transformations in the life of a child, it's clearly absurd to think that we can always approach the job—or the child—in the same way.

A mother who had brought her son to my office was trying to ease his apprehension about talking to a counselor. In her reassuring mother's voice she tried to calm his fears, saying, "It's okay, sweetie pie. Mommy's going to be just outside, okay? If you need mommy you just call for me, okay? I'm not going anywhere, angel. Mommy will be right here." The boy sitting in my office was 17 years old. I wanted to tell him, "Listen, I don't know what you're in here for, but I'm on your side. That lady's a nut!" No wonder he seethed with anger toward his mom. She was treating this near-adult like the small child he'd been more than 10 years ago.

Parents who don't adjust their approach to coincide with their child's developmental growth can expect to see increasing levels of resentment and bitterness in their kids.

How Do You Hug a Cactus?

One distraught mother told me, "He doesn't want me to love him. When I try to reach out, he all but bites my head off. How am I supposed to love someone who doesn't want me to love him?"

I certainly understand her feelings, but I'm so glad that my heavenly Father didn't stop reaching out to me during all those years when I acted like I didn't want His love. My behavior may have indicated that I didn't want anything to do with God, but my soul was crying out for the God who made me, loved me and died for me. My words and my outward façade contradicted the reality of my heart's longing. The same is most likely true for your child. He may act as if he hates you, but down deep he longs to have a deep, intimate connection with his parents. So I urge you to commit to repairing the relationship whether or not your teen wants it, accepts it or reciprocates.

At the same time, it's important to be honest about your own feelings. After years of bearing the brunt of a child's wrath, many parents find it hard to be in the same room with the child, much less reach out in compassion and pursue a renewed relationship. If this description fits you, it's time to stop beating yourself up with guilt. Your feelings are normal and appropriate, given what you've been going through. Just because your feelings of affection have been battered into retreat by your teenager's hateful ways, that doesn't mean your deep-seated commitment of love and devotion has fled the scene. You may not like your child at the moment—and understandably so—but your love for her remains.

Bottom line: No matter how your child responds or what emotions you're wrestling with, it is God's will that you seek reconciliation. Even if your child rejects your peace offerings or you are not exactly in the mood to buddy up to the little monster, your responsibility remains the same. You have been given, by God, the ministry of reconciliation. In 2 Corinthians 5:18, Paul states, "All this is from God, who reconciled us to himself through Christ and gave us the ministry of reconciliation." While we tend to read this verse in the context of reconciling a lost world back to its Heavenly Father, these words are just as true when it comes to your responsibility to your family. God calls each of us to reconcile our children back into a loving relationship with their heavenly Father. And that road to reconciliation begins with making every effort to reconcile our hearts with the hearts of our children.

You see, regaining control of an out-of-control teen is not simply about discipline strategies; it's also about reestablishing God-honoring relationships between family members. So if repairing your relationship with your teen is the key to regaining control in the home, where do you start?

Ride on the Peace TRAIN

Most parents of defiant children would love to jump on board the Peace Train (for those of you old enough, a slight tip of the hat to Cat Stevens). With that in mind, I'll use the acronym TRAIN to highlight five specific strategies to help you begin repairing your broken relationship with your oppositional child and ride the Peace Train all the way to reconciliation.

Time

Certain well-worn pieces of advice for parents, like the importance of spending time with their kids, have become common clichés. How do you spell love for your children? T-I-M-E. What is the greatest gift you can give your child? T-I-M-E. But here is another truism: Truisms become truisms because, well, they tend to be true. Spending quality time with your defiant teen is one of the most effective strategies for reestablishing the ruptured relationship. Notice that word *quality*. Some would argue that there is no such thing as quality time, only quantity of time. They believe that quantity and quality amount to the same thing, so the goal is simply to spend as much time as possible in the presence of your child. In their view, what happens during that time is not nearly as important.

I, on the other hand, firmly believe in the concept of *quality* time. One dad who brought his daughter to my office for help with her defiant behavior told me that the issue of time was not a problem in their relationship because he spent almost every night at home with his kids. His daughter, however, said that she seldom ever saw her dad and described their relationship as very distant.

Trying to understand their contradictory perspectives, I asked the mom to describe their evening routine. Here's what she said: "The kids and I get home about 4:30, and they go immediately to their rooms to begin their homework while I get dinner ready. My husband gets home about 6:00, just about the time dinner is done. He grabs a plate to take into his home office, where he continues working. The kids come down about that time, grab plates and head back to their rooms to eat while I sit down in front of the TV to eat my meal. The kids stay in their rooms either doing homework, chatting on the phone, socializing on the computer or playing video games while my husband spends most of the evening working in his office. I clean up the kitchen, do a few household chores and then watch some more television before going to bed."

It became apparent that the dad's view of the home environment was more than slightly out of touch with reality. The mom's description made it clear that simply being in the same house, the same car or at the same activity doesn't mean we are interacting a meaningful way with our kids.

Quality time involves interaction, communication and in some way exercising the relationship. This doesn't mean engaging your child in thought-provoking philosophical, political or spiritual discussions every time one of them steps within a five-yard radius. But at some point during the day you need to "check in" with your kids.

Married couples frequently hear cautions against leading "parallel lives." Rather than living two separate lives under one roof, they need to share one life together. This means knowing each other's daily routines and being aware of a spouse's current pressures, struggles or triumphs.

Each partner expresses interest in the other person's day, because they view those details are an integral part of their life together.

The same can be said of our families. A family is not simply four separate lives existing under one roof, but *one* family sharing *one* life together. Yet all too often, family members are disconnected from one another. I've talked with more kids than I can count who confess to having no idea what their father does for a living. They literally have no clue. How can this be? How can a child not have some understanding of what his father does for 8 to 10 hours a day? But then, how many fathers could give an accurate description of what takes place in his child's life on a typical day?

Checking in with your child doesn't mean grilling her about how she spent each moment or giving him the third degree about how late he slept. It's as basic as finding out how the test went, what the coach said or what happened during his latest foray into World of Warcraft. Just a casual checking in goes a long way toward uniting the lives under your roof.

Another great way to experience quality time with your teenager is to schedule specific time periods to be alone together. This may seem daunting if your child is extremely defiant, but I encourage you to press on. Find something to do, somewhere to go, some activity to engage in—*together*. This should be a deliberate span of time designed to break out of your usual mode of interaction. Worn-out parents of defiant children tend to go into autopilot, in which most discussions with their kids consist of telling them "No," "Stop it" or "Be quiet." We literally become No-Stop-It-Be-Quiet Machines. To help break this pattern, try seizing these one-on-one times as opportunities to avoid using those words. Deliberately choose to remain positive and upbeat during your time together. Remember: We can do all things through Christ who gives us strength!

Since it may be tempting to think you don't have time for close encounters of the teenage kind, I'd like you to take out your Blackberry right now and look at your schedule. Where do you spend your time? How many hours each week are reserved for interacting on a personal level with your child? I'm going to guess the majority of your time is devoted to work, friends, hobbies, household responsibilities? None of those things are necessarily bad, but are they more important than your child?

Investing quality time is every parent's first and best step in repairing the relationship with a defiant teen.

Reduce Negativity

Pessimism is one of the distinguishing characteristics of parents of extremely defiant children. Cynicism and negativity are natural byproducts of the constant mental and emotional warfare these parents fight every day.

As believers, however, we cannot give in to this "natural" tendency for pessimism. Christians, by the very nature of our faith, should be optimists. We need to be like local Chambers of Commerce who are unabashedly upbeat and optimistic about their cities. I'm thinking of the mayor who was asked how the recession was hurting his town. He replied, "Recession? We're not in a recession. But I will admit that we are having the worst boom in many years." That's the kind of optimism I'm talking about!

The writer of Hebrews tells us that "faith is being sure of what we hope for and certain of what we do not see" (11:1). As people of faith, we believe that where there is God, there is hope. And the last time I checked, God was omnipresent, in all places at all times—even the homes of extremely defiant teens.

Matthew 6:33 is a theme verse for many of the parents I work with. In this section of the Sermon on the Mount, Jesus was encouraging his listeners to have faith and not worry about all the things that non-believers always worry about. Why? Because God has promised to meet our needs. Jesus states, "Seek first his kingdom and his righteousness, and all these things will be given to you as well." He gave his listeners an alternative to worry and anxiety: *Seek first the kingdom of God.* If you do that, then all of your fears and reasons for pessimism will be taken care of. Your heavenly Father knows what your family needs, and if He is sought *as the first priority,* He will meet those needs. That's a promise straight from God's Word.

Fear is the opposite of faith and negativity is the opposite of hope. Our relationship with God brings great hope. Hebrews 6:18-19 asserts, "We who have fled to take hold of the hope offered to us may be greatly encouraged. We have this hope as an anchor for the soul, firm and secure." Do these verses describe your current outlook toward your defiant child? Can you honestly say that the hope offered in your relationship with Christ greatly encourages you in your current family situation?

Trust me—I work daily with families overwhelmed by constant struggles with a defiant teen, so I understand how difficult it can be to look beyond the everyday vitriol and conflict to see the greater picture that God remains in control. But let's reflect for a moment on the story of Peter walking on the water with Jesus in Matthew 14. The outspoken disciple wanted to demonstrate his absolute trust and devotion to his Lord, so he asked if he could come out onto the water where Jesus was walking. Jesus bid him come, and Peter climbed boldly out of the boat. Things started out just fine. But then he took his eyes off Jesus and began focusing on the tumultuous wind and waves surrounding him. Peter got scared and began to sink.

This is a perfect example of what happens in many homes with exceptionally defiant teens. As parents, we become so overwhelmed and frightened by the shockingly rebellious behavior of our child that we take our eyes off of the sole Source of our hope. When we take our eyes off of Jesus—His presence, His power, His love, His will, His control and His compassion—we begin to sink, lose hope and become as pessimistic as any other parent who doesn't have the hope of Christ in their life.

Perhaps another biblical example will help put things in perspective. The prophet Samuel went to the house of Jesse because God said that's where he would find the next king of Israel. Initially drawn to Jesse's oldest son, a strapping young man, Samuel heard clearly from God that he must keep looking. After considering all of Jesse's sons, he did not find the future king among them. The puzzled prophet asked Jesse if he had any more sons hidden away. Surely God had not made a mistake in sending him here! Jesse acknowledged that there was one other son, who was out watching the sheep in the field, but he couldn't possibly be the one the prophet was seeking. He was the runt of the family. Still, Samuel wanted to see him, so Jesse summoned David to come home (see 1 Sam. 16:1-13).

When God looked upon David, He didn't see the youngest and scrawniest of Jesse's sons; He saw the next king of Israel, a man after His own heart. If we can look on our kids the way God looks at us, we will find reason for great hope. Rather than being distracted by their current negative behavior or discouraged by their present defiant demeanor, we can look at them through the eyes of Christ. Then we will see them not for who or what they are now but for who and what God has called them to become. In Christ, our negativity is washed away by the power and purposes of God. Let this hope be an anchor for your soul.

Act Against Stereotype

Did you know that your rebellious teen has stereotyped you? I can guarantee that when you walk into a room, she already knows what you are going to say, how you are going to act and what decision you are going to hand down. She has lived with you long enough to know your mood, your priorities and your temperament. This is why so often when you attempt to teach her a valuable life lesson, she responds with, "Blah, blah, blah." She's heard your routine so often that she knows it by heart.

A stereotype is a simplified conception or belief someone holds about a particular person or thing. To put it directly, your teen has simplified you. To her, you are simply mean, or stupid, or unfair, or uncaring, or you don't listen, or you're a hypocrite. It doesn't matter what you say, because she already knows all about you—and she couldn't possibly find you more boring or irrelevant. We touched on this in the last chapter when we explored the adolescent narcissistic fantasy. Self-absorption convinces your irrational teen that she can't learn anything from you. She knows exactly which people have anything worthwhile to say, and you don't make the list.

As frustrating as this is, it's important to recognize that some perceptions kids have about their parents are based in reality. If your son claims that you never listen to him, it could be that you seldom do. If your daughter accuses you of always yelling at her, maybe you do raise your voice more than you should.

Robin's parents brought her to my office because they were concerned about her failing grades and newfound tendency to defy their authority. After several sessions, Robin tried to articulate her despair over her relationship with her mother. "She never listens to me. She just doesn't care about me or my life." So I gave Robin an assignment for the week: "Go home, ask to speak with your mother, then request her help in thinking through a problem you're having at school or with a friend. Let's see how she responds." The following week, Robin entered my office with the same defeated demeanor as usual. When I asked how her homework went, she said that she had brought an issue up with her mother and they had spoken together about it for several minutes. I listened to her description of her mother's advice and told her that I thought that sounded like a great conversation. "So why do you still seem so depressed about it?" With tears in her eyes, Robin looked at me and said, "The whole time I was talking with her she never stopped looking at the computer screen. It was like I wasn't even there." This mom said all the right things and probably went to bed that night feeling good about connecting with her daughter. In reality, her actions and body language spoke louder than her words.

Whether or not you agree that your child's stereotype of you is accurate, a powerful step toward reconstructing your relationship is to acknowledge the negative pattern your child perceives and purposely work against it. If you know that your child feels as if you never listen to him, then purpose to listen carefully to what he has to say. If your daughter believes that you don't care about her, then take every opportunity to demonstrate your concern and to spend time with her. Remember: Whether the perception is true or false matters less than demonstrating to your child that you take the criticism seriously and are willing to do whatever it takes to remove this impediment to the relationship.

Interest in Your Teen's World

In the pursuit of their own sense of independence and identity, teenagers have created their own "world" of existence. Most parents simply do not understand the complexity of this world, or the power it holds over their teenagers.

For example, Molly came into my office, concerned that her daughter was acting in some disturbing ways. Previously outgoing and vivacious, Nikki had grown sullen and seemed to have withdrawn from her social circle. Molly felt compelled to get her daughter professional help after noticing several three-inch cuts on Nikki's upper right arm that looked self-inflicted. When she brought Nikki in the following week, I found her to be a cute and engaging young girl, but she was initially reluctant to divulge what was troubling her. That changed when we hit on the topic of her Facebook page. The picture that slowly emerged from that conversation was that of a young life shadowed by intense threats, harassment and uncommon cruelty. It seems that Nikki had angered another young lady at her middle school by flirting with her boyfriend. The other girl responded by using her Facebook page to systematically annihilate Nikki's reputation and any hopes of ever having a normal social life at that school again. When Molly learned of the situation, she assured her daughter that those were just words. "None of your true friends would ever believe what's being said on that MyFace page."

She actually said "that MyFace page."

Nikki screamed, "You just don't understand!"

And she was right. This mother clearly did not understand the power of a teenager's private world.

In October 2006, this private world claimed the life of young Megan Meier, a sweet 13-year-old girl from Missouri, who committed suicide after being bullied and belittled online.[2] It's almost impossible to overemphasize how complex and painful the private world of teenagers can be.

Chap and Dee Clark conducted some groundbreaking research into teen life in America, which they share in their wonderful parenting book *Disconnected: Parenting Teens in a MySpace World.* Of this private teen world they write, "It all begins with the community that adolescents claim is the only safe place they have, the underground world where adults are not welcome—the 'world beneath.'"[3]

We parents may not understand or be welcomed into our kid's "world beneath," but it is incumbent upon us to make every effort to learn as much as we can about it, because this is where our teens spend so much of their time. Now, don't get me wrong. I don't believe we have to immerse ourselves in all things teen and wear ripped T-shirts from Abercrombie & Fitch or count down the days until the next Kanye West concert, but we should have some working knowledge of the adolescent experience. Some parents take great pride in being ignorant of the teen subculture, as if they are in some way too holy or pure to be bothered with knowing the name of today's most popular rap artist. They seem to believe that knowing what is shown on MTV in some way implies approval of the content. Nothing could be further from the truth.

Parents of teenagers should proactively keep abreast of teen culture because this knowledge offers a window into their child's heart, mind and driving interests. The Bible tells us in 1 Chronicles 12:32 that when David was forming his army, he called upon the men of Issachar because they "understood the times." And since they understood the times, *they knew what to do*. I truly feel that God calls parents to *understand the times* so that they will *know what to do,* how to connect with their kids. I believe it's important for Christian parents to know where this year's *Real World* on MTV is being filmed, who's hosting *Saturday Night Live* this week and what's hot in fashion, music and technology.

But your teen's world involves more than cultural trends. It's critical to know who your child is hanging out with and what's going on in her broader social circle, such as who's going out with whom. These personal connections serve as the flashpoints for a teen's joy and pain, and by keeping up to date on the latest social news, you gain huge insight about the state of your child's heart.

How on earth can you ever glean this type of information? It takes numerous *non-judgmental* conversations with your kid—not prying in order to punish but listening in order to learn.

Your teen's private world is impacting his life whether you like it or not. Being ignorant of it is not something to be proud of. I believe it shows a callous disregard for much of what represents your teen's identity. By summarily dismissing all of youth culture, your teen gets the feeling that you are dismissing him as well. But simply showing that you care enough to know some of what is going on in his world demonstrates that you love him enough to connect on his terms.

Not Every Moment Is a Teachable Moment

This final car on the Peace TRAIN to a repaired relationship with your teenager stands in contrast to one of the greatest parenting truths ever: the importance of seizing upon normal, everyday experiences and using them as "teachable moments" in your child's life. I remember as a young parent—and when I say "young," I mean that Sarah was born when Beth and I were only 21 years old—listening to Dr. James Dobson as he cautioned his radio listeners to not squander the opportunities God provides to teach our kids the lessons that will mold their character. Failure in school, being let down by a friend, not making the team, breaking up with a boyfriend, not getting the scholarship—all of these, he said, are teachable moments that wise Christian parents use for the betterment of our children. And I couldn't agree more.

Some parents, however, take this concept to an unhealthy extreme by turning *every* moment into a teachable moment. The number-one complaint I hear from kids is, "My mother nags me constantly. I hate that!" Now, I understand that many of these haphazard young ones need certain reminders throughout the day, but many times I think these teens have a valid complaint. I occasionally ask a parent to back off the guidance and direction for a week or so as we attempt to address the breach in relationship. Often, the parent simply cannot force him- or herself to do it.

In one session with Mary and her 16-year-old son, Thomas, we all agreed that she would try to curb her nagging over the course of the next week, allowing Thomas to suffer the consequences of any responsibility that he might miss. When they reported back the next week, "I told you so" was written across Thomas's face. They both agreed that Mary didn't do well at reducing the number of times she nagged at her son. "What was I supposed to do? Just let him fail?" she asked defensively. "If he's doing something he shouldn't, it's my job as a parent to point it out."

This mother's line of reasoning is well taken, but can also be exaggerated to an unhealthy level. Some parents get so caught up in rebuking, correcting, teaching, coaching, instructing, molding and guiding that little time is left to simply relate to their child as a person. As mentioned earlier, sometimes all our kids hear from us is "No," "Stop it" and "Be quiet." We never ease up. We never give it rest. We never stop with the incessant criticism of their behavior. To tell you the truth, if I lived with someone who constantly nagged and corrected me, I'd be mad at them too—and so would you, I imagine. Yes, we are instruments in the hands of God to mold and shape our children into the young men and women He created them to be, but—as in most situations— moderation is the key. If we constantly correct, teach and point out flaws, then the effectiveness of those tools is diminished. But when we use those parenting techniques sparingly, they are much more effective.

So how do you relate to your child if you're not incessantly correcting and instructing? That's quite a challenge, isn't it? I wonder how long it's been since you saw your child as a human being instead of a moldable lump of clay. Stepping out of your role as the constant corrector will free you to interact with your child as you would any other friend or family member. I'm not suggesting that you abandon your parental responsibilities and become just another friend; I want you to consider the value of sometimes just easing up and enjoying your child's unique personality and insights. Converse like loved ones. Share stories. Laugh at life's circumstances. Relate to each other like normal people. Letting your teen know that you see her and appreciate her as a real, authentic person in her own right and not just the object of your endless instruction will go a long way in helping re-establish a healthy relationship.

Fasten Your Seatbelt

If you ride the Peace TRAIN to reconciliation, you will discover that the ride can be quite bumpy at times. Trying to restore a relationship with someone who doesn't share that goal can be a challenge. If the levels of antipathy in the home are high, it will be difficult to work toward reconciliation with your child. In fact, this part of the equation is, in many cases, more difficult than establishing the boundaries, determining the consequences and enforcing those boundaries with consistency.

But I can assure you that you'll never regret taking this journey. Persistence is the key to success. As Winston Churchill said to encourage the British nation during the Nazi bombings of World War II, "Never give in. Never give in. Never, never, never, never—in nothing, great or small, large or petty—never give in except to convictions of honour and good sense. Never yield to force; never yield to the apparently over-whelming might of the enemy."[4] We have been called to love our kids whether or not they want that love, respond to that love or return that love. Determination, persistence and perseverance in pursuit of a re-stored relationship will drive us to never give up. And if we adopt the mantra that we will relate to our children the way God relates to us, then the author of Hebrews leaves us with these words of encouragement:

> In the beginning, O Lord, you laid the foundations of the earth, and the heavens are the work of your hands. They will perish, but you remain; they will all wear out like a garment. You will roll them up like a robe; like a garment they will be changed. But you remain the same, and your years will never end (1:10-12).

God never gives up. He remains as a rock solid source of love and stability, and so should we.

To Sum It Up

Rest assured that the firmness of your family rules is not the cause of your teen's rebellion. In all likelihood, a breach in the parent-child rela-tionship has created space for your child's defiance. And it is imperative that you take responsibility to initiate a reconciliation.

You can ride the Peace TRAIN to restored relationship with your child by putting into practice five key strategies. First, do whatever it takes to spend as much quality time with your child as possible. Quality time involves interaction, communication and in some way ex-ercising the relationship. Second, reduce negativity. As believers, we cannot give in to the "natural" tendency for pessimism that afflicts so many parents of exceptionally defiant children; we are people of faith who are filled with hope in God. Third, act against stereotype. You can surprise your child by acknowledging the negative stereotype she perceives in you and purposely work against it. For example, if you know that your child feels that you never listen to her, then purpose to listen carefully to what she has to say. Fourth, maintain an interest in your teen's world. We parents may not understand or be welcomed into our kid's "world beneath," but it is incumbent upon us to make every effort to learn as much as we can about this world in which our teens spends so much time. And finally, it's vital to recognize that not every moment is a teachable moment. Some parents get so caught up in rebuking, correcting, teaching, coaching, instructing, molding and guiding their children that little time is left to relate to them as worthwhile and unique individuals.

A Quick Follow-up

Do you remember Robin? She was the young girl whose mother made her feel invisible by not making eye contact with her during a discussion. Sadly, this was not an isolated incident with Robin's mom; it was the norm. Robin desperately wanted a closer relationship with her mom, and her mother was oblivious to the whole problem. I was able to meet with the mother on several occasions after that and was encouraged by her willingness to take some responsibility for the disharmony in her home; she was very much open to change. Within just a few weeks, their relationship was noticeably improved, and that healing was the first step in Robin's own personal journey toward healing and a change in her defiant behavior.

HAVE A SEAT ON THE COUCH

1. How difficult is it for you to spend quality time with your children, especially your defiant child? Why? What immediate steps do you feel you could implement to address this issue?

2. Do you believe that you have fallen victim to excessive negativity when it comes to your defiant child? How have you seen your attitude change over time? Do you believe it's possible for you to release that negativity and bitterness and instead look at your child through the eyes of Christ?

3. How do you think your child has stereotyped you? What specific actions could you take to act against that stereotype?

4. How much of your teen's "world beneath" do you know about? Do you think it's important to have a grasp of that world? Why or why not? What are some ways to keep abreast of your child's culture without being voyeuristic?

5. Do you find that the only interaction with your child is in the form of correction or instruction? How long has it been since you've just hung out as two people who love each other? Do you believe that your and your child's bitterness make this impossible? What might be your first steps in "normalizing" your relationship with your defiant teen?

THE QUESTION OF CONTROL

When speaking of family dynamics, there can be only one answer to the question of control: *Control cannot be in question.* In this regard, the home, as a functioning organization, is much like a sports team, a ship at sea or a successful company. Leadership is crucial. Someone has to call the shots, and the determination of who holds that power is not up for a vote. Any uncertainty about who's in control usually leads to chaos.

Let's talk about the word "control" for a moment. For many people, this word conjures up negative visions of one person exercising oppressive, smothering manipulation of another individual, as in "control freak." But when I speak of control in the home, I mean it in a much more positive, appropriate sense. A teacher who retains control of her class is not being oppressive; he's providing a healthy environment for learning. A policeman who takes control of a situation is not smothering freedom but ensuring safety. A pitcher who has control of his curveball isn't scheming for world domination but positioning his team for a win. Like many other positive things in life, it can be abused and become a negative, but for our discussion, control should be viewed as a proper relational element essential to every healthy family.

Several months ago, I met with a family whose control problem had created a mess in their home. The father and mother sat on the love seat across from me, and the couple's 11-year-old son and 15-year-old daughter sat on the couch to my left. When I shut the door to the counseling room, it was like sounding the bell in a boxing ring—all four fighters came out swinging. The daughter led off with a jab about how stupid it was that she had to be there. The son jumped in with a loud complaint about how his sister was sitting too close to him. The father yelled at the kids to be quiet, and the mother struck back by yelling even more loudly that the father shouldn't be yelling at the children.

As this four-way match entered its fifth minute, I reached into the drawer next to me, took out a bottle of Advil, popped a couple, and then turned to face the fracas. After several attempts, I finally got the attention of the contenders long enough to ask a simple question: "Would the adult in the room please stand up?" I didn't care which family member rose to the challenge; it could even have been the 11-year-old, for all I cared. I just needed one member of this family to agree to act the part of a level-headed adult.

This family was on the verge of chaos because of a complete lack of leadership and modeling of proper behavior. Each person treated the others as though they were equals. The children showed no deference to their parents; the parents demonstrated no sense of authority over their children or mutual respect for each other. No one followed any normal rules of social etiquette, and the kids felt free to act in whatever way might get them what they wanted.

This is a worst-case scenario for parents. When we lose control in our homes, we may as well echo the words of that great theologian and psychologist Willie Nelson: "Turn out the lights . . . the party's over!"

The Void Will Be Filled

Back when I was a youth minister, one of my youth workers gave me a baseball cap with two bills. I made sure to wear it on most of our group outings. The front of the cap read, "I'm their leader . . . which way did they go?!" That humorous cap highlighted a key principle of maintaining control: True leaders do not chase after the crowd; the crowd follows a true leader. A person who has a vision, communicates that vision and encourages those around him or her to share in that vision is a leader others find easy to follow.

I'm sure that at some point, you've found yourself in a business setting where the supervisor didn't have a clue. As my dad used to say, the person "didn't know 'Come here' from 'Sick 'em.'" So no one followed the supervisor's orders or respected him as a leader. Such people may be in charge on paper, but in reality they are relegated to insignificance. Situations like this become uncomfortable for everyone involved. (If you've ever seen the sitcom *The Office*, then you get the general idea.) Because the person in charge doesn't know how to get things done, it's left to whichever of the subordinates are most capable of assuming the mantle of leadership. How does this scenario go over? Not particularly well, right? The supervisor gets mad because his employees do not respect him or his decisions, and the employees get mad at being forced to do the work of an inept supervisor. I'm sure you'll agree there's not much possibility for achieving success or satisfaction on this "team."

Now let me ask you a tough question: How successful would you say your home is? Are you in charge only on paper, while your family deems your leadership insignificant or inept?

Consider this axiom of business management: Where there is a void in leadership, others will move in to fill that void. And what is true of business is also true of our homes. Where there is a void in parental leadership, the children will move in to fill that void. If the children can disregard the opinions, advice, instructions and commands of the parent without consequence, then those children—the supposed subordinates in the family—feel emboldened to exercise their own power and fill the void left by the parent's impotence.

How Our Kids Conduct a Coup d'État

The term *coup d'état* refers to a sudden change in government, usually by force. It's basically a rebellion to overthrow those in charge. Even if the phrase is unfamiliar, I'm sure you understand the principle.

After years of talking with exceptionally defiant teenagers, I'm convinced that they employ deliberate strategies to gain control in the home. They purposely act in ways that discourage, frustrate and weaken parental resolve, in order to undermine the parent's control of the family. By taking away a parent's control, the teenagers, in essence, have gained the control themselves. A *coup d'état* has happened before our very eyes.

Let's take a look at four strategies defiant teenagers use to gain control in the home.

Passive Resistance

When Eric's parents brought him into my office, his dad explained that the teenager had agreed to come but had assured them that he would not speak to me under any circumstances. Lots of kids make similar claims, but most open up in a session or two and do just fine. With this in mind, I began to probe Eric's defenses by asking some rather harmless questions. "So Mom and Dad forced you to come in, huh?" No response. "You know, we can talk about everything except you and your family. Would that be okay?" Still nothing. After several similar attempts on my part, Eric mimed that he would like a pencil and paper. I handed them to him, and he wrote, "I'm sorry that this may seem rude, but I told my parents that I wouldn't speak and I'm a man of my word." I nodded my head in understanding, and then spent the next 48 minutes reading *Sports Illustrated*.

Rest assured that we'll come back to Eric a little later in the book, so you can see how his pattern of silence was eventually broken. For now, I simply want to focus on his behavior as an example of passive resistance. He was not a get-in-your-face screamer. He would simply retreat into his room and not come out. He would refuse to speak to those who had offended him, and no amount of coaxing or persuading would alter his stated course of action.

Bear in mind that passive resistance is not the same as passive-aggressive behavior. Both involve covert, as opposed to overt, resistance to authoritative directions. In both behaviors, the individual may demonstrate sullenness, inflexibility or procrastination—the person fails to accomplish an assigned task. One of the distinguishing characteristics of passive-aggressive behavior, however, is that it is mostly unconscious. For example, a husband who doesn't want to go over to his in-laws' for a family dinner might fail to get home on time from the golf game, drag his feet getting ready, be unable to find the clothes he wants and end up being so late that his wife finally goes without him. Now he can claim, with a clear conscience, that he had every intention of going to the gathering, that he loves her parents and that she is unreasonable to claim otherwise. But what was the end result? He didn't go to his in-laws'.

A passive resister, on the other hand, *intentionally* uses sullenness, inflexibility and procrastination to *intentionally* resist doing what he is asked. He has a clearly defined goal of coercing his parents to give up and give in. Back in the '60s and '70s, students would sometimes launch a "sit-in" to protest whatever they saw as an objectionable school policy. A bunch of students would walk into the administrative building of their university and sit down. They didn't fight or scream or make a huge scene. They simply committed themselves to remaining seated until the local officials listened to and gave in to their demands. Just to get all of these kids to go home and return things to normal, many authorities acquiesced. These protesting students had a specific goal in mind and executed an intentional plan to accomplish their objectives.

So it is with exceptionally defiant teenagers who apply the strategy of passive resistance. Their premeditated goal is to exasperate their parents until they become so put out, so tired of the constant struggle, that they finally just give in to the child's demands. When this happens, the teen has successfully wrested control of the home away from the two people that God ordained to be in authority: the parents.

Relentless Debate

Grace had made up her mind. Daughter Caroline's reign as teen queen of the house was over. No more Mrs. Nice Guy. This mom's days of being a pushover were at an end, effective immediately. Caroline would not be going to that party tonight, and Grace felt confident knowing that simple, solid logic was on her side: She didn't know the parents in that home, she didn't like the kids who would be there and she couldn't trust her own daughter to stay out of trouble. After thinking through each point, she stepped into her daughter's room to deliver her verdict: an unequivocal no.

About one minute later, Grace's rock solid resolve began to fade under the onslaught of debate:

Caroline: What do you mean "no"? You have no right to ruin my life! You've let me go to tons of parties when you didn't know the parents. Why start being so ridiculously strict now?

Grace: Well, that may be true, honey, but I know those kids that are going to be there, and you know I don't approve of how they behave.

Caroline: You have no idea who's going to be at that party! Half the youth group from the church is going to be there. Do you think all of them are drunken sex maniacs? Geez, you're so stupid sometimes!

Grace: Well, young lady, that may be true, but you have not been making good choices of late, and I'm just not sure I can trust you not to get into trouble, no matter who's going to be there.

Caroline: Am I grounded right now? Hello?! No! Do I still have my cell phone? Yes! If I was that much of a troublemaker, don't you think I'd be paying for it by now?

And now for the grand finale, the not-so-subtle dagger thrust into her mom's heart . . .

Caroline: Mother, I know you feel guilty because you drove dad away. Well, take a look in the mirror: You're doing the same thing to me. If you want to grow old alone and never see me or your grandkids, just keep it up. Dad said you were a control freak, and he was right!

With tears in her eyes, Grace retreated to her bedroom, and Caroline went to the party.

Relentless debate is another purposeful strategy employed by a defiant child to wrest control away from a parent. This strategy is straightforward: The teen will be incessant, relentless and uncompromising in his effort to destroy and dismantle every argument put forward to justify a decision. His plan is to pseudo-intellectually thwart his parents, point by point, until they eventually run out of arguments and give in to the defiant child's "logical" line of reasoning. When a child can argue his way around his parents' decisions or rules, those parents have lost control of the home.

Domination by Fear

While passive resistance relies on subtle behaviors to seize control from parents and relentless debate involves a more cerebral approach, domination by fear is like your teen using a sledgehammer to post a notice on your bedroom door.

I can usually identify victims of domination by fear soon after they step into my office. I always spend my first session with the parents, before meeting with the child, to get a baseline understanding of exactly what is going on in the home. Near the close of the session, most parents offer a fairly accurate picture of the level of resistance I can expect from their child. I know we're in trouble when they say something like, "Well, this all sounds great, but how are we ever going to get him to come? I mean, there's no way we could ever get him here." Once parents lose the ability to take their child places he may not want to go—such as the doctor, school or the dentist—we can say with certainty that they are no longer in control of the family.

When I first met Tim's parents, they weren't just afraid that they might not be able to persuade him to come to counseling; they were actually afraid of *him*. With his long history of violence and physical intimidation, this ruthlessly aggressive, highly explosive, perpetually ticked-off 15-year-old struck fear in the hearts of every member of his family. His parents knew that when push came to shove, Tim would push, shove and anything else he felt like doing to get his way. If they confiscated his cell phone, he stole theirs. If they revoked his television privileges, he ripped the cable box out of the wall so that no one in the house could watch TV.

To say that Tim's family worried constantly about triggering hidden landmines and setting off new explosions would be an understatement. They all tried their best to keep him happy and avoid provoking his rage. Needless to say, this child controlled his home and held every member of his family hostage with his short-fused temper and fiery rage. Tim had established himself as the "alpha male" of his home and would fight anyone who attempted to remove him from his position of prominence.

Leading by Default

Some young people have been masters of their households right from the start. From practically their first moments on earth, their parents have kowtowed to their every whim. Did you know that the word "kowtow" actually refers to the act of kneeling and touching the forehead to the ground in—get this—*servile deference*? What a great word-picture for how some parents allow even their small children to totally control the home. They treat their offspring with all the reverence that a slave affords his master.

Dr. Robert Shaw notes that one of the most troubling words in a parent's vocabulary is "okay." As in, "It's time for bed . . . okay?" "Let's go get cleaned up for dinner . . . okay?" "It's time for you to do your homework . . . okay?" From the child's perspective, the parents are soliciting approval and agreement for what sounds like suggestions rather than instructions. It seems that many parents, from the days of toddlerhood right through the teen years, are "running their needs" past their kids, as though the children need to sanction the request.

When Beth and I lived in a student-housing complex during my grad school years, one neighbor couple had two small children about the same age as ours, both under four. When we first got to know them, we discovered that their philosophy of child rearing was markedly different from ours. I remember Beth and I visiting with them outside the door of our apartment one night about 10 PM. We had tucked our kids into bed a couple of hours earlier, but this couple's children, as usual, were rampaging all over the property. By this time of night, they were fussy, irritable and in no mood to "play well with others." I remember the kids screaming and fighting with each other, pausing only occasionally to demand that their parents go get them something to eat. To our shock and dismay, each time a demand was made, one of these beleaguered parents would dutifully get up, go inside and come back out with a bowl of some sugary cereal. The kids would scarf it down without a word of thanks, then the chaos would continue. Beth and I must have been staring at them as though they were aliens from another planet, because the husband just grinned at us and said, "Kids. What are you going to do?" Although we resisted the impulse to say so, Beth and I knew that there *was* something that he could do. He could be a parent.

Here's another example of the child who ends up leading by default. Jim was sitting in my office because his 12-year-old son, Scott, was becoming increasingly defiant. Jim didn't really want to be there, but his wife, Sarah, had insisted. As we talked, he expressed concern that his young boy was listening to dark heavy metal music known as "death metal." He found it troubling that Scott seemed to be depressed, wore nothing but black clothing and seemed obsessed with death and suicide. Then Jim made a comment that I knew I would use in a book if I ever wrote one: "I hate that he listens to this kind of music. I think it's bad for him and probably makes his depressed moods even worse, *but who am I to tell him what music he can listen to?*"

Such a statement would be comical if it weren't so utterly tragic. It took every ounce of my self-control not to jump out of my chair, grab this guy by the shoulders and shake him while ranting, "Who are you to tell him what music he can listen to?! You're his *father,* that's who!" The problem was that Jim had never assumed his God-given role as the leader, guardian, mentor and protector of his family. In other words, he'd never truly been a father. Jim had never viewed himself as the authority in his boy's life, and now his son was paying the price for that passivity. Scott was left to lead himself, to serve as his own authority by default. And no 12-year-old is ready for that responsibility.

Parent the Way God Parents

Those are just four strategies that defiant teens employ to take control away from their parents when they sense an opportunity. Remember: Where there is a void in leadership, kids will move in to fill that void. So how do we prevent such a void from developing? How can you make sure that the question of control is never in question in *your* home?

The answer is as simple as parenting our kids the way that God parents us. I say it at the risk of sounding clichéd, but I'm convinced that it's absolutely true. Our goal should be to parent our children the way that God parents us. Which brings us to the question, how does our Heavenly Father parent us? I believe that God relates to us as His children primarily through six attributes of His character.

Let's look at each of these attributes and consider how they can be interwoven into our own parenting styles. I realize that this may sound like a theology lesson, but I truly feel that understanding this will go a long way in helping you regain control of your home from your defiant teen.

God Is Loving

So many passages in the Bible point to the great love of God, but 1 John 4:8 sums it up: "Whoever does not love does not know God, because God is love." *God is love.* That straightforward declaration encompasses all His other characteristics. God not only demonstrates love for us, He is the embodiment of what love is all about. Earlier in his letter, John declares, "How great is the love the Father has lavished on us, that we should be called children of God. And that is what we are!" (1 John 3:1). The Father lavishes love on His children. He isn't stingy with His affection; He offers it freely and generously.

How is this lavish love demonstrated? Paul does a great job describing the kind of love God shows His children in the thirteenth chapter of 1 Corinthians. From that passage, we know that God expresses His love in many ways, including by being patient and kind, and not ever being self-seeking or easily angered. Of course, God's greatest display of love was in sending His only Son to die for us on the cross. Our Father's example should inspire us to lavish this same kind of love on our children, putting their needs above our own and sacrificing on their behalf.

God loves His children unconditionally, and so should we.

God Is Forgiving

We know from the Bible that forgiveness is another manifestation of our Father's parenting style. Psalm 86:5 says, "You are forgiving and good, O Lord, abounding in love to all who call on you." First John 1:9

reassures us that "if we confess our sins, He is faithful and just and will forgive us our sins and purify us from all unrighteousness." God's actions from Genesis to Revelation demonstrate a Father's forgiveness given freely to his children.

An important point for us to remember is that God's forgiveness of our sins was not dependent on our deserving or earning it. We do nothing to deserve forgiveness, yet our Heavenly Father freely gives it anyway. Why? Because that's God's nature; that's just who He is.

God forgives His children unconditionally, and so should we.

God Is Accepting

The early history of the Church records a struggle over just what kind of a faith Christianity would be. You can read Galatians for an account of the dispute between those who believed all Christians must adhere to Jewish law in order to be accepted by God and those convinced that people could be saved only by grace through faith, not by good works. Who won? We should know by now that grace always wins in the end. Acts 10:35 reassures us that God "accepts [people] from every nation who fear Him and do what is right."

This characteristic of our Father was revealed clearly in the life of His Son when Jesus spoke to the outcast Samaritan woman at the well, ate with tax collectors and other sinners and invited rough—and most likely foul-smelling—fishermen to join Him in His mission. Jesus not only demonstrated acceptance in His actions, but He emphasized it as a significant theme in His Sermon on the Mount:

> You have heard that it was said, "Love your neighbor and hate your enemy." But I tell you: Love your enemies and pray for those who persecute you, that you may be sons of your Father in heaven. He causes his sun to rise on the evil and the good, and sends rain on the righteous and the unrighteous. If you love those who love you, what reward will you get? Are not even the tax collectors doing that? And if you greet only your brothers, what are you doing more than others? Do not even pagans do that? (Matt. 5:44-47).

Acceptance of all people is fundamental to the character of God, which means it should be fundamental to our character as parents. Acceptance of your child doesn't mean approval of her negative behavior; it simply means holding your arms wide open for the time when your wayward child turns her heart toward home.

God accepts His children unconditionally, and so should we.

God Is Holy

The vast majority of believing parents would wholeheartedly agree with what I've just said. When I speak to parents around the country and ask them to describe how God parents us, they never fail to acknowledge His love, forgiveness and acceptance. The problem, as I see it, is that too many parents stop there; as a result, they fail to understand, as Paul Harvey said for so many years, the rest of the story. As Christian parents, it is crucial that we also recognize God as being holy, just and sovereign. These less-emphasized characteristics of our heavenly Father play just as vital a role in our relationship with our children.

I will not bore you by reciting all the verses that describe the holiness of God; suffice it to say, Scripture clearly highlights this as an attribute of our Heavenly Father. In fact, the Bible refers to holiness more than 900 times, suggesting the importance God places on this characteristic. In the New Testament, we find a heavy emphasis on practical, daily holiness as a vital part of every believer's life. The Greek word translated "holy" means something akin to "Christ-likeness." So the idea of holiness is to be like Christ, both inside and out. The author of Hebrews states, "Make every effort to live in peace with all men and to be holy; without holiness no one will see the Lord" (12:14). So living up to the standard that God gave us in the life of Christ is not something *suggested* by our Heavenly Father; it is something that He expects and demands.

How can our parenting reflect the characteristic of holiness? We should set a standard that our children are expected to live up to. We should outline a pattern of behavior that we don't just *suggest* they adhere to, but that we actually *require* of them. Does this sound harsh? Jesus Himself said, "From everyone who has been given much, much will be demanded" (Luke 12:48). Did Moses bring down the Ten Suggestions from Mount Sinai for the people of God or the Ten Commandments? From the very beginning, God has set boundaries for us and demanded that we obey them. And by "very beginning" I mean the Garden of Eden. Even in paradise, God set a boundary that He required His children to respect. When they violated that boundary, they suffered the consequences for their behavior.

God requires His children to follow a standard of behavior, and so should we.

God Is Just

The concept of justice includes both *protecting the rights* reserved for individuals living in a particular society and *enforcing the consequences* of violating the standards and expectations of that society. For example, a criminal who is punished for his crime is receiving justice for his actions. And when the courts determined that Rosa Parks had every right to sit in the front of that bus in Montgomery, Alabama, in 1955, she also received justice. I guess we could say that justice is God's way of making sure people get what's coming to them, both in a negative and a positive sense. In fact, Scripture teaches us that the Father's attribute of justice is what necessitated His Son's death on the cross, as Paul explains in Romans 3:25-26:

> God presented him as a sacrifice of atonement, through faith in his blood. He did this to demonstrate his justice, because in his forbearance he had left the sins committed beforehand unpunished—he did it to demonstrate his justice at the present time, so as to be just and the one who justifies those who have faith in Jesus.

Our Heavenly Father is eternally committed to enforcing justice, even at the cost of His Son's life.

We can be no different in our parenting. Justice demands that we enforce appropriate penalties for any negative action. If your child violates a known boundary, it is your responsibility to bring consequences for that action if you intend to reflect the complete character of God in your parenting. But as stated earlier, justice is not limited to punishment for doing wrong. By simple virtue of their place in your family, your children reap an enormous number of blessings, such as food, clothing, shelter and material and financial benefits—not to mention being a part of a group of people that love each other, support each other, believe in each other and defend each other. It is a reflection of our justice and the justice of God that children not only are held to certain expectations but also receive all the rights and privileges that come with being a member of a family.

God demonstrates justice to his children, and so should we.

God Is Sovereign

The term "sovereignty" refers to the divine authority by which God rules His creation. Psalm 135:6 puts it simply: "The LORD does whatever pleases him, in the heavens and on earth, in the seas and all their depths." We also read in Psalm 24:1 that "the earth is the LORD's and everything in it, the world and all who live in it." The totality of Scripture teaches that God is in everything and rules over everything. Bottom line: God is in control.

Okay, since we are not all-knowing or all-powerful and we didn't bring all that exists into being, how can we mere mortals reflect the sovereignty of God? I believe strongly that parents represent the physical presence of God in the lives of our kids. By having Christ alive within us, we reflect the fullness of who God is (see Col. 2:9). Therefore, we must do everything in our power to get ourselves out of the way and allow all the fullness of Christ shine through us. To parent like God, we need to accurately reflect all His attributes, including love, forgiveness, acceptance, holiness, justice, and—I believe—His sovereignty. Obviously, we can't claim to know everything and rule over everything, but in our child's life, we are to be in control. The buck stops with us.

As a kid, more times than I can count, I would ask my dad why I had to do something and he would respond—say it with me—"Because I say so." I just hated that! It was like he was just lording his authority over me and gloating while he did it. At the time, I swore that if I ever had children, I would never, ever say that to them. I'm guessing that

Sarah was maybe a week old before I looked in her crib and said, "Because I said so, young lady. That's why." Initially I felt awful for betraying my childhood self every time I channeled my father and let those words come out of my mouth. But upon further review, I changed my opinion. "Because I said so" is a completely legitimate reason for a child to obey her parent.

I think most parents can tell the difference between a child who truly wants to understand the "why" behind an assigned task and a child who is just being obstinate. Instead of entering into a protracted debate about the appropriateness of our request, if it is determined that the child does not lack understanding, then I believe that we more accurately reflect God's sovereignty by explaining to the child that simply knowing his parent has asked him to do something is reason enough for him to comply. Since it is a true representation of the character of God for Him to be in control of all creation, it is a true representation of our responsibility as parents to be in control of our homes.

God remains in control at all times, and so should we.

It's Not Either/Or—It's Both/And

In contemplating the multi-faceted character of our Heavenly Father, we've looked at what we might call His "grace side," which shows his love, forgiveness and acceptance, and we've examined what we'll call His "holy side," which reflects his holiness, justice and sovereignty. My experience in working with families leads me to believe that many parents tend to major on one of these sides or the other. Either they focus primarily on grace and forgiveness, or they concentrate on holiness and justice.

Grace-focused parents tend to sacrifice justice in the name of forgiveness. When they set a limit, they often back away from enforcing it because they worry about being too harsh. The grace-focused parent might ground a disobedient child for three days, but then reduce the grounding to only two days as a reward for good behavior.

One set of parents came to me for help in dealing with their defiant 14-year-old daughter. The girl had run up a phone bill over $100 in one month; as a consequence, they took her cell phone away. I asked the dad how long they kept her phone. He explained that since the girl seemed so repentant for her actions, he let her have it back . . . after only one day.

Noted pastor and theologian Dietrich Bonhoeffer, in his book *The Cost of Discipleship*, introduced the phrase "cheap grace." He wrote:

> Cheap grace is the preaching of forgiveness without requiring repentance, [it is] baptism without church discipline, Communion without confession, absolution without personal confession. Cheap grace is grace without discipleship, grace without the cross, grace without Jesus Christ, living and incarnate.[1]

As parents who want to demonstrate the full character of God, we should protect the value of grace, preventing our kids from seeing it as something "cheap" and easily obtained, by employing it as the exception and not the rule.

In contrast to grace-focused parents, justice-centered parents are all about law and order. Their actions say that it is more blessed to punish than to reprieve. These by-the-book parents rarely take circumstances into account. The law is the law, and they will exact retribution for every violation.

Mark, a justice-centered parent who believed in challenging his kids to their best possible performance, told his son Chris that any grade below a *B* was completely unacceptable, and he set clear consequences for failure to achieve. If Chris ever brought home a report card with a *C*, he would be grounded for a month: no time with friends outside of school, complete revocation of phone privileges and absolutely no communication via the Internet.

Chris was working his hardest to keep up in his Advance Placement Algebra course. He spent hours on homework every night, went to school early to meet with his teacher for tutoring and took advantage of any extra-credit work the teacher offered. After all that effort, he still received a 79 on his report card, just one point shy of the 80 his father required. Mark explained how disappointed he was by Chris's failure to meet expectations and gave his son the full punishment that had been promised.

Obviously, the rule was intended to deter Chris from getting lazy about his academics. Laziness, however, had nothing to do with his Algebra grade. He had tried as hard as any kid could, but that type of math just didn't click with him. Despite his protests of unfairness, his parents remained unmoved and enforced the letter of the law, confident that they were right in standing by their word.

As parents striving to represent the full character of God, we help our kids value the rules and the accompanying consequences when we execute them with wisdom, understanding and mercy. Arbitrary rules or blind enforcement of them only diminishes a child's belief in his parents' love and in the worth of trying to meet their standards.

Whether we lean naturally more toward grace or toward justice, it is important to understand that parenting like God is not an either/or proposition; it is a both/and. To only show His justice is just as much a misrepresentation of God's character as reflecting only His grace. The trick is to fence in our homes with holiness, justice and sovereignty, but to fill them with love, forgiveness and acceptance. This, I believe, is how we remain in control as parents. We establish boundaries for our children, setting reasonable, godly standards and enforcing them justly and fairly no matter what resistance our children puts forward.

Discipline, however, must be communicated in love, bound up with forgiveness and rooted in unconditional acceptance of who your child is: a child of God and a child of yours.

To Sum It Up

Parental control of the home is not a negative or oppressive thing but a positive aspect of every healthy family. But kids will employ numerous strategies to wrestle that control away from their parents, including passive resistance, relentless debate, domination by fear and leading by default.

To avoid creating a leadership void that kids will gladly leap into, parents need to brand on our frontal lobes the importance of parenting as God parents us. This means reflecting His whole character, including His love, forgiveness and acceptance, *and* His holiness, justice and sovereignty.

A Quick Follow-up

I would like to catch you up on Grace and her daughter, Caroline, who apparently had a black belt in debate. You'll remember that Grace was so bowled over by Caroline's constant, aggressive arguments that the child usually got what she wanted. Grace developed a contract for her defiant daughter and included in the contract a special section on keeping a debate going even after the mother had made a final decision. She initiated a catch phrase to signal that the discussion was over. The phrase was "The discussion is over." Quite original, I think. But it worked like a charm. From then on, whenever Caroline pushed a discussion with her mother, Grace simply said, "This discussion is over." If Caroline mentioned the topic after that, it cost her the use of her cell phone and computer for four days. Within the month, her debating, negative behavior was all but eliminated. Caroline and her mom certainly had other issues that we continued to work on over time, but the Great Debater was forced into retirement.

HAVE A SEAT ON THE COUCH

1. I had a dad just this week tell me, "I'm very uncomfortable telling my kids what to do. I don't like controlling people." Do you ever feel this way? Do you, in some way, see control as a negative aspect of a home? Why or why not?

2. Which of the four strategies that kids use to gain control of a home do you see used most in your family? What does your child do specifically to implement his or her strategy?

3. We are to be parents to our children the way our Heavenly Father is to us, right? So, which of the six attributes of God mentioned in the chapter do you find the easiest to demonstrate? Why?

4. Do you find it difficult to balance these attributes in your home? How can you strike a balance between being more grace-focused *and* more justice-centered?

5. Do you feel as if the parent who can balance all these attributes of our Heavenly Father and reflect them to his or her children is almost like a mythical creature? Do you believe it's possible? Why or why not?

IF WE KEEP DOING THE SAME THINGS THE SAME WAY . . .

The factor that most often propels people into counseling is a desire for change. They identify some area in which they are less than satisfied with themselves or their families and seek a counselor's help in moving toward change. Sometimes, however, these individuals don't initially understand that *their own behavior* is what needs to change. They may be focused on dealing with symptoms or on "fixing" what is wrong with the people in their lives rather than recognizing their own need to jettison negative attitudes and actions and take on healthier, more productive thoughts and behaviors. It's been said that babies are the only people who like change, and it's certainly true that many of the families I work with are eager for solutions but resistant to change.

Ron and Stacy came to counseling when their 16-year-old daughter's behavior became unbearable. She was exploding frequently in violent anger, sneaking out of the house, having sex with her boyfriend and smoking weed, even in their house. Ron and Stacy agreed that something needed to be done and appeared eager for change. But every strategy I suggested was met with a ready excuse as to why that wouldn't work in their home with their daughter:

- "We've tried that. It doesn't work."
- "She doesn't care if things are taken away."
- "We don't want our rules to make her stand out among her friends."
- "There is no relationship left for us to work on, so why try?"
- "I don't want to be my child's warden! I'm her mother."
- "I would never punish her like that. That's way too extreme."

I wouldn't say that I was exasperated with them; I understood that they were parenting the only way they ever had, in the only way they knew how. But I also knew that to have any hope of bringing peace back to their home, they had to at least be open to the possibility of change. I tried this approach: "You've heard that insanity is doing the same thing, the same way, expecting a different result? Well, you guys seem to want to keep doing the same things in the same way while wanting a different result. And there's not going to be one. You have to be open to doing different things, in a different way, if you want to attain different results. Look at it this way," I continued. "Parenting in the way that comes naturally to you is what brought you here to my office."

Ron and Stacy finally came around to the importance of addressing their daughter's behavior in a whole new way. In a few short weeks, they were thrilled with how their family had been reshaped for the better.

I'm guessing that the idea of altering your parenting approach feels a little intimidating to you as well. Breaking out of the pattern of how you've always done something is bound to feel awkward. But let's say that you own a car company, but the cars rolling out of your plant don't work. The doors won't close properly, the engines keep stalling and the tires frequently fall off. As the owner, you aren't satisfied with the finished product of your manufacturing plant. So what do you do? Do you continue to follow the same steps and keep pumping out the defective cars, hoping that one day they will magically change and all the flaws miraculously correct themselves? Probably not. As a wise owner, you examine your manufacturing process to determine the exact point where the problems develop, and then you change the process at those points to fix each problem. By changing the process, you change the quality of the finished product.

In much the same way, parents of defiant children have to be willing to change the process if they want to change the outcome of their efforts. In this chapter, we are going to discuss several essential tactics for parenting an oppositional child. If you recognize any of these elements as missing from your parenting approach, then those need to be on your list of things to change. If you have a defiant teen in your home, I believe the following strategies are crucial to returning peace to your family. But even if you are parenting a more "normal" teen who doesn't exhibit extremely defiant behaviors, including these elements in your parenting approach will be helpful.

Choose Your Battles and Win the Battles You Choose

How many times have you heard someone assert this key parenting principle: "You gotta choose your battles"? At least a million times, right? But truer words were never spoken. We can't treat every issue as though it is equivalent to all others. Certainly, a teenager's failure to tuck in his shirt when dressing for church should not earn the same parental response as his hiding a bong in his baseball card box. Both may be issues, but they are not equivalent issues. I'm not saying that smaller problems shouldn't be dealt with in some capacity, only that it would be a mistake to confront each concern with the same intensity and vehemence.

If you go to the mat over every behavioral misstep your child makes, you are going to be one burned-out, frustrated and exhausted parent. This is especially true if you're dealing with an exceptionally defiant child. You could get dizzy just considering all the potential battles, much less waging war over each and every one.

It takes wisdom to determine which battles to fight and which to let slide. Where can you gain that wisdom? You got it—this kind of wisdom is another gift promised by our Father. James 1:5 assures us, "If any of you lacks wisdom, he should ask God, who gives generously to all without finding fault, and it will be given to him."

How often have you felt certain that you lacked the wisdom you need as a parent? How many times have you thought to yourself, *I have no idea what the best thing is to do here.* God is one step ahead of you, offering exactly what you need. He knows how difficult it is to parent a child. He even knows how difficult it is to parent an extremely defiant and rebellious child, and He knows that you need a supernatural portion of His wisdom to do His will in those difficult situations. That's why He has instructed you to simply *ask.* Just ask your heavenly Father for the wisdom you need; He promises that it will be given, and given generously!

If you ever feel outmatched and unprepared for the challenges of parenting a defiant teen, then your need for God's wisdom should drive you to your knees every day. But be warned: Don't ask for God's wisdom if you don't really want it. Don't ask if you aren't committed to trusting Him and acting on His direction. In fact, that's what James goes on to warn in the very next verse: "But when he asks, he must believe and not doubt, because he who doubts is like a wave of the sea, blown and tossed by the wind" (1:6). So don't complain if the wisdom you receive from God is not exactly what you want to hear. Don't turn your back on this gift from God simply because it requires more than you want to give. If you ask God to help you determine which battles to focus on and He gives you the wisdom to make that determination, then you are accountable to act decisively with that wisdom, to confront your child and engage in whatever fight your heavenly Father deems worthwhile. Conversely, if He says to let it go, then you need to back off—even if it means biting your tongue to prevent the words of criticism from erupting out of your mouth.

Dove-tailing from the discussion of control in the preceding chapter, once you have chosen to fight a particular battle, then losing that battle is out of the question. You must win. Period. No questions asked. The legendary coach of the Green Bay Packers, Vince Lombardi, is often attributed with saying, "Winning isn't everything; it's the *only* thing." Those words frequently are pointed out to highlight the negative impact of a "win at all costs" philosophy, and I largely agree with those criticisms. Even so, a parent's attitude about winning carefully selected battles with a defiant teen should reflect the essence of this over-zealous axiom. The cost of losing is simply too high.

What would happen if a person caught speeding knew that if she yelled and screamed long enough, the police officer would eventually concede to her demands and let her drive off without consequences? What if a criminal could shout out threats and intimidate the trial judge into letting him go free despite his obvious guilt? Surely chaos would break out. We would cease being a nation of laws and become a society ruled solely by the survival of the loudest and the strongest. Well, just as our society can't exist if the governing authorities failed to deal effectively with those who break the rules, neither can our families. Once we have determined which battles to engage in with our oppositional kids, we have no choice but to win.

But, you ask, *how can I assure victory in those battles?* Good question. The answer is to incorporate the rest of this chapter's essential tactics into your parenting strategy.

Give Your Child a Reason to Change Her Behavior

Some kids are just naturally compliant. They do what is right, try their hardest and put forth their best effort in every situation. They work hard, do the extra credit and go to bed early without being asked because they want to be rested for the big test the next morning. And they do this with no prompting from teachers, coaches or parents. It seems to be part of their genetic makeup to seek the approval of the authority figures in their lives. Does that description match your experience as a teenager? It certainly doesn't fit mine, but the fact is that the vast majority of us were not significantly rebellious while growing up.

These kids are *internally motivated.* They truly want to do the right thing and succeed in all their endeavors. To do otherwise just wouldn't compute with them. Randy Agnew, one of my best friends in high school, was just such a teenager. Randy, an overachiever if there ever were one, not only excelled in football, making varsity before the rest of us, but was also the leading candidate for valedictorian. He was close to a model child at home. I remember once trying to convince Randy to sneak out with me and do something that God has allowed me to forget. He gave me every reason in the book as to why it was a terrible idea and pointed out that if we were caught, all of life would come to an end. Trying to get Randy to break out of his good-guy role was like trying to convince Billy Graham to take up smoking. I finally persuaded him to go with me, but he had a miserable time and regretted his decision. Randy was internally motivated to be compliant and do the right thing.

Others of us relate more to the *other* group of kids—those who are naturally more insubordinate. It seems to be their nature to push the limits, test the boundaries and question the authority figures in their

If We Keep Doing the Same Things the Same Way . . .   95

lives. They'll eventually comply with instructions, but only after every objection has been raised, every excuse offered and every boundary pushed. These kids have to be *externally motivated*. Because the desire for compliance and success is not "bred" into them, they need a reason to comply. This is where we parents come in. It is our job to give them a reason to change their behavior. We need to provide an external source of motivation because the internal one is not yet functioning.

I remember Marsha, the mother of a rebellious 16-year-old, going on and on about how her son spoke to her in such a horribly disrespectful way. "He's rude to me, yells at me, and calls me profane names all the time. Just last night, I told him to stay at the table and finish his dinner with the rest of his family. He told me that I could go !@#$% myself, and that I was a $%^&!" I hope you are among those who can't imagine your child saying something like this, but for many parents, this scene is all too familiar. Appalled by this young man's behavior, I asked Marsha what punishment her son received for speaking that way. She said, "I was too upset to deal with him then, and when things calmed down, I didn't want to rock the boat and stir it all up again. So I guess he didn't receive any punishment." My response was, "Then why wouldn't he keep treating you that way? If he is able to cuss you out in front of the entire family and suffer no negative consequences whatsoever, what motivation does he have to stop behaving like that?"

It's extremely unlikely that an exceptionally defiant kid will suddenly find the "on" switch to his personal moral compass and be internally motivated toward proper behavior. He has to be given an external reason to comply. Most of the time, this external motivator takes the form of sufficiently frightful consequences, in which the child is given the choice to continue the negative behavior or suffer the penalty. Parents who don't provide their teens with an ample reason to change a negative behavior have no hope of curbing that behavior.

Bad Choices Must Result in Bad Consequences

How does God teach us? Certainly, He speaks to us through the Bible. But when it comes to teaching His children life lessons and prompting change, I believe that our heavenly Father employs another tool as well: More than anything else, God uses the natural consequences of our sinful behavior to teach us about what is right and wrong. In a general sense, our Father uses the natural boundaries that He has set in place to instruct us in the way we should go.

Sex is a great example. The negative consequences of promiscuous sexual activity are legion. A young lady who engages in casual sexual encounters has better-than-even chances of contracting a sexually transmitted disease, getting pregnant and then choosing to have an abortion, damaging her relationship with her parents, hurting her relationship with God—and the list could go on and on. But what happens when this young lady stays a virgin until she marries, marries a virgin and then they remain faithful to each other for as long as they both shall live? That's right: It's all good. If she has sex by the Book, she has no reason to worry about likely negative consequences. If we engage in sex the way prescribed by the One who invented it, then all these risk factors are eliminated. By following God's will, we remain safe, but when we choose to rebel and live outside His protection, bad things can happen. Our bad choices tend to result in negative consequences.

The natural connection between choices and consequences affects every area of life. If you don't study for a test, you won't do very well. If you slack off on a job, you'll get reprimanded—or worse. If you make too many trips to Krispy Kreme, you'll look like me. If you cheat on your taxes . . . well, that's too horrible to even imagine. But you see what I mean. As a general rule, God uses the natural consequences of our negative behavior to teach us how to live. In fact, the author of Hebrews spells this concept out for us:

> And you have forgotten that word of encouragement that addresses you as sons: "My son, do not make light of the Lord's discipline, and do not lose heart when he rebukes you, because the Lord disciplines those he loves, and he punishes everyone he accepts as a son."
>
> Endure hardship as discipline; God is treating you as sons. For what son is not disciplined by his father? If you are not dis-

ciplined (and everyone undergoes discipline), then you are ille-
gitimate children and not true sons. Moreover, we have all had
human fathers who disciplined us and we respected them for
it. How much more should we submit to the Father of our
spirits and live! Our fathers disciplined us for a little while as
they thought best; but God disciplines us for our good, that
we may share in his holiness. No discipline seems pleasant at
the time, but painful. Later on, however, it produces a harvest
of righteousness and peace for those who have been trained by
it (12:5-11).

How long has it been since you have read those verses? Can you
hear the voice of God Himself speaking those words of encouragement
to you?
Hebrews teaches us here that God sometimes allows negative
events in our lives to discipline us. He does this for our good, so that we
can share in His holiness, so that we can reap the benefits of living ac-
cording to the standard He has set for us. How else are we going to
learn? An even better question is, how else are our children going
to learn? We set boundaries for our children because it is good for
them. We make sure that they suffer bad outcomes for their negative
behavior because we want to help mold and shape them into the people
God has created them to be. Although such discipline is painful for
them and many times difficult for us, it has to be done.
I see another vital point in this passage: God talks about disciplining His children because He loves them, noting that it may be painful
for a time but that it produces a harvest of righteousness. This includes our kids, because our children are God's children. He disciplines our children because He loves them and wants what is best for
them—and He knows how to bring that about. Most of the time, parents are instruments in God's hands to carry out discipline and implement His will in the lives of their kids. But what if the parents fail to
provide the discipline that the heavenly Father wants for their child?
What if parents get in the way of God loving His own children?
Certainly, we would never deliberately do that. But how often do we

prevent our children from experiencing God's best by not allowing them to suffer the natural and God-desired consequences for their poor behavioral choices?

God disciplines those He loves, and so should we.

Make Your Word Your Bond

Joe and Carol had run out of ideas for dealing with the increasingly defiant behavior of their son, Colby. As they described to me their home environment and how they, as a couple, handled different discipline situations, they confessed their most significant parenting failure: "We are both terrible at following through with what we say we are going to do," Joe acknowledged. Carol agreed: "We talk a good game, but when it comes down to actually making good on our threats of punishment, we normally just back down. And what's worse is that Colby knows it! I don't even think he believes us anymore when we say we're going to punish him." And she was right—her son *didn't* believe them anymore.

You know the old story about the boy who cried "wolf." He repeatedly sounded a false alarm about impending danger, just to get a response from the villagers. Then when the wolf actually did arrive and the boy cried "wolf," no one believed him. His word had become meaningless. Jesus Himself said, "Simply let your 'Yes' be 'Yes,' and your 'No,' 'No'; anything beyond this comes from the evil one" (Matt. 5:37). As believers, our word has to mean something. When we say we're going to do something, we need to do it, because we gave our word. It is a matter of honesty, integrity and being a person of honor.

Most of the Christians I know would never dream of breaking their word to a friend or telling their fellow employees a bald-faced lie. Why? Because we want to be known and trusted for our upright and ethical behavior. At the same time, few of us give much thought to what it means when we fail to follow through on a promise to our kids. For some reason, our moral, ethical and Christian obligation to the truth stops at the kitchen door. No wonder most kids simply roll their eyes when a parent says, "You're going to be in big trouble when we get home!" They don't believe a word of it. Their parents have made so many idle threats that their reputation as an authority figure is shot. Their words no longer carry warning but have been relegated to insignificance.

When you tell your child that she will suffer a specific consequence because of her behavior, you are making a promise. You are declaring your intention to do something. If you don't follow through, then you are breaking that promise. You are lying to your child and demonstrating that your word is meaningless. Your integrity is undermined, and you have lost the moral high ground in your attempts to encourage her to be honest in all her dealings.

Doing what you say you're going to do is important for every parent, but when you have an exceptionally defiant child, it may be the one of the most critical aspects of your parenting strategy. Your child has to know that you mean what you say, or he'll have absolutely no incentive to listen to you. So I encourage you to take a tip from that great model of parenting virtue, Horton the Elephant, who said, "I meant what I said and I said what I meant; an elephant's faithful—one hundred percent!"[1] Do you say what you mean and mean what you say? Are you faithful, 100-percent?

Remember that Parenting Is Not About You

One of the greatest opening lines of any book ever has to be the first line of Rick Warren's *The Purpose Driven Life*: "It's not about you."[2] That's how he summed up the starting point for finding God's purpose in your life. Well, what's true of our lives in general also happens to be true of our lives as parents. It's not about us. So often our interactions with our kids center on us and our feelings. Our parenting decisions and discipline choices tend to be about our needs and how we feel about a situation. Do any of these comments sound familiar?

- "I'm so disappointed in you."
- "I've had it with you, young man!"
- "How dare you speak to your mother like that!"
- "I did not raise you to act that way."

- "Your father is the pastor! Did you ever stop to think about that?"
- "You have gotten on my last nerve!"

When a father named David described for me something that happened with his 16-year-old son, Zach, I recognized it as a scene that could have been videoed in the homes of most of my clients. After being told he couldn't go to the movies with his buddies, Zach had come to the dinner table in a foul mood. In addition to the usual sulking, he was taking out his anger by sniping at his siblings and talking back to his parents. When David asked his son to pass the salt, Zach finally crossed the line by telling his father what he could do with the salt shaker. David reacted pretty much as you might expect: "That's it, buster. You are outta here! I've had all I'm going to take of your smart mouth, so go to your room. Now!"

Although David's frustration is understandable, let's take a closer look at exactly what his words communicated to his son. He told Zach to go to his room. Why? Was it because he had violated an established boundary of respectful behavior and banishment to his room was the established consequence for such behavior? That's not the reason Zach's dad gave. David's basis for sending Zach to his room was, "I've had all I'm going to take of your smart mouth." This teen was sent to his room not because he violated a family rule but because his dad was mad and wanted revenge. Instead of teaching Zach the importance of respect, David's lesson to his son was, "If you tick me off, you'll be sorry." In this dinner-time encounter, David focused not on Zach and his choices, but on himself and his frustration level. Because similar scenes play out in countless homes on a daily basis, it's no wonder kids sometimes see their parents as personal enemies bent on making them miserable.

So if parenting is not about us, what is it about? Simply put, parenting is about being used by God to mold and shape our kids into the image of Christ. Parenting is about our children and about their heavenly Father. It is about doing whatever is necessary for growth, maturity and discipleship to happen. When our kids make poor choices, our disciplinary strategy should focus not on punishment and punitive responses, but on our children being reconciled to God.

During the years our kids live at home, we are the primary tools God uses in shaping our children toward sanctification. If you've spent much time at church, I'm sure that you have heard this word bandied around quite a bit—but what does it really mean? Bottom line: The New Testament concept of *sanctification* involves growing in holiness, or growing in Christ-likeness. This process begins at the time of our conversion and continues until we close our eyes on this earth and open them in glory.

As parents, we are the instruments God uses during our kids' first 20 years or so to accomplish this process of molding, or sanctification, in their lives. We don't actually carry out the sanctification; that's God's job. Every difficulty our kids face, every tragedy they experience and every poor decision they make is an opening for God to mold them closer into the image of His Son, into the fulfillment of what He created them to be.

We participate in the process at His will. When we look at our children and the parenting process through the eyes of our Heavenly Father, viewing our temporary roles in light of His eternal and sovereign purposes, our outbursts of frustration and anger seem sort of petty and insignificant, don't they?

Recognize Yelling as a Sign of Weakness

Are you one of those people whose frustration level can be measured by the decibels of your shrieking? If so, you're not alone. Just like Zach's dad, many parents resort to yelling as their default coping mechanism during highly stressful parenting situations.

Most likely, if you're a yeller, your childhood home often echoed with yells, as well. One of your parents was probably an old yeller . . . (sorry, I couldn't help myself). Yelling tends to be a *learned response* to anger, stress and frustration. If your parents conducted themselves in this manner during your childhood, it sort of comes naturally to do the same with your own kids. But here's the problem: If you tend to yell when frustrated, stressed or angry, then you're liable to blow out your vocal cords when parenting an exceptionally defiant teen. Because stress, frustration and anger are not just occasional occurrences in a house with an oppositional teen—they are a way of life.

I'll never forget the mom whose first words in my office nearly shattered the glass of my lava lamp: "YOU WOULDN'T BELIEVE MY DAUGHTER!!! SHE YELLS ALL THE TIME!!! EVERY TIME SHE'S UPSET, SHE JUST STARTS YELLING AT THE TOP OF HER LUNGS, AND I DON'T KNOW WHY!!!"

"Wow," I said. "I wonder where she picked up that nasty habit?"

The first step in reducing verbal conflict in your home is restraining your own bad habit of yelling when upset. As tempting as it may be to let escalating emotions twist your volume knobs to maximum levels, you need to realize that parents set the emotional tone of the home. If your manner of interaction is calm, civilized and respectful, then your family is likely to reflect that example. But if instead you choose to crank up the volume and intensity, then just as you learned to yell from your parents, chances are that your children will learn the same coping mechanism from you. How can you, in good conscience, ask your kids to remain calm if you're not willing to do the same?

Some parents defend their habit of raising their voices by saying, "You don't know what it's like in our home. I have to yell just to be heard." These parents are trying to direct my attention to the negative behaviors of their children, but all I hear is that they are losing or have already lost control of their home. If you have to yell to be heard, something is wrong. Again, authority figures like policemen or judges don't have to yell to get their point across. Why? Because they hold the ultimate power. They are in control and don't have to prove a thing. Yelling sends a message to your child that her behavior has the power to unnerve you to the point of provoking an outburst. I can't tell you how many kids sit in my office bragging about how they can set their parents off! They take pride their ability to frustrate their parents to the point that they lose control and have a screaming fit. This is why yelling is a sign of weakness in a parent, not a sign of power. You may think that you're laying down the law, taking control of the situation or demonstrating your power by yelling, but in all reality, your lack of restraint reveals that your child holds the reins.

Present a United Front with Your Spouse

I feel so strongly about this that we devote an entire chapter to this issue a little later in the book, but for now we'll put it on the list of parenting essentials in a home with a defiant child. Nothing undermines the parenting process more effectively, nothing exacerbates the tension in a home more rapidly and nothing fans the flame of defiant behavior more alarmingly than two parents at odds with each other over how to deal with a rebellious teen. Let's briefly examine several factors that can lead to division and dissension between parents when it comes to the discipline strategies for an oppositional child.

I wrote my dissertation on how raising a defiant child affects the marriage relationship of the parents. The main finding of my research was shocking. Nearly every couple that participated in the study had one thing in common: a conflict-avoidant, passive husband. We'll look at this in more detail later, but having a father who is engaged, involved and who sees himself as an equal partner in the parenting process is absolutely key to successfully parenting a defiant child. When a dad checks out, the child's defiant behavior kicks in.

So many dads just want to do their jobs, come home, provide for their families and be left in peace. Their "peace through appeasement" strategy sounds something like this: "Look, let's just let him download the album. He's right—all his friends own it. If this will calm things down, let's just let him get it." You'll notice that nowhere in this dialogue is there any mention of what is good for the child, what the morally correct choice is or what would be pleasing to God. This dad is concerned with how quickly the tension in the home can be resolved so that he can be left in peace. I believe this is a huge mistake, because the active, caring involvement of the husband and father is essential to successfully parenting a defiant child.

Another factor that leads to a disruption of parental unity is a fundamental difference in how each spouse views the discipline process. As I've mentioned before, we tend to parent the way we were parented. Couples who come from different parenting backgrounds tend to hold differing views about consequences, boundaries and what is and is not appropriate behavior. It is critical that you and your spouse talk through these differences and then agree on the discipline strategy to be implemented in your home. When your approach to parenting conflicts with that of your spouse, you send a confusing message to the kids and you risk alienating your best partner in the fight against rebellion.

Finally, while most children employ the basic "divide and conquer" tactic at one time or another, defiant kids have elevated this approach to an art form. When the oppositional child intentionally points out how your take on a situation conflicts with that of your spouse, don't take the bait. You already know that your child is going to attempt to pit you against each other, so why on earth would you act as if you are reading from the child's script? Simply refuse to go there.

Now, sometimes your child may have a point. Maybe you feel that your spouse has overreacted or has misunderstood your teenager's position in a particular disagreement. Even so, one spouse should never, ever, under any circumstances abandon the other in front of the children. If you disagree, take it to another room, get your heads together and come back with a united front. It may be necessary for one parent to apologize and reverse a decision. Whatever the case, it is crucial that you never openly side with your defiant child over your spouse.

This may sound overly simplistic or unrealistic, but I encourage you to be willing to make the necessary changes in how you parent your kids, even if it feels awkward and uncomfortable. Getting Mom and Dad together is absolutely essential.

Don't Be Your Kid's Friend—Be His Parent

Okay, I'll make this one short and sweet, but it definitely needs to be mentioned. Many parents react to an overly defiant child by trying to "connect" with him, to "understand" him or to "be there for him." They often try to befriend the child by being lax about enforcing consequences, negating the disciplinary decisions of the other parent behind his or her back or even openly taking the child's side in family arguments. As we've just discussed, presenting a united front is a nonnegotiable in dealing with a defiant child. But the temptation to connect with your child as a personal friend presents a whole different set of problems.

One 40-year-old mom once tried to explain to me the close relationship she had with her daughter. She said, "Maggy is my best friend! And she'll tell you that I'm her best friend too."

As gently as I could, I had to respond, "I understand what you're trying to say, but I'm afraid that's just gross. It's disturbing to me that a 40-year-old would have a 14-year-old best friend, and no normally developing 14-year-old needs to have a 40-year-old for a best friend. I'm glad you two are close, but that's just inappropriate."

It's very simple: You can't be your child's friend and parent at the same time. Why? Because the two roles are drastically different. Parents have to make tough decisions, discipline when necessary and set forth guidelines that will irritate the child. That's what parents do. Friends function as equals. They offer advice that you can choose to take or leave. And they back off when you ask them to.

Now, there comes a time when being your child's friend is certainly appropriate. My three kids are all in their 20s, and I count them among my closest friends on earth. But our relationship didn't morph into friendship until they were well into adulthood. By valuing the importance of your unique role as a parent during the teen years, you're helping your child grow into an adult you'll be proud to call your friend down the road.

To Sum It Up

In this chapter, we emphasized the need to be open to change, because doing the same things in the same way while expecting a different result is just crazy. We also discussed eight essential parenting tactics that, if not already part of your strategy, can serve as your outline for change:

- **Choose your battles and win the battles you choose.** You'll be exhausted if you invest the same level of effort in fighting every problem. But once you decide a battle is worth fighting, you can't afford to lose.

- **Give your child a reason to change his or her behavior.** Children who are not internally motivated to do the right thing, make the right choices, and always do their very best need parents to provide them with incentives to make a change for the better.

- **Bad choices must result in bad consequences.** Just as our heavenly Father teaches us through consequences, parents must make sure that their defiant child always suffers negative consequences for negative behaviors.

- **Make your word your bond.** Follow-through is crucial when dealing with a defiant child. You must say what you mean and mean what you say.

- **Remember that parenting is not about you.** Parenting decisions and discipline choices should not be centered on your desires and how you feel, but on how God is using you to mold and shape your kids into the image of Christ.

- **Recognize yelling as a sign of weakness.** Parents may think that yelling is taking control of a situation and demonstrating their authority, but their lack of restraint actually demonstrates loss of control and emotional weakness.

- **Present a united front with your spouse.** To counteract a defiant teen's tactic of "divide and conquer," parents must be on the same page, must be working in the same direction and be supportive of each other.

- **Don't be your kid's friend—be his parent.** Trying to "buddy up" with a defiant teen can damage your current and future relationship with your child. Your child needs you to set boundaries, enforce rules and make tough decisions.

A Quick Follow-up

You'll remember Marsha and her very defiant and verbally abusive son.
I'm sad to report that things never really got better for them. We tried
to implement a contract, but Marsha was unable to make the hard decisions to enforce it. We discussed specific strategies for confronting
her son's out-of-control behavior, but to no avail. When the family
eventually stopped coming in, my heart hurt for this single mom. She
wanted help. She wanted things to be different in her home, but when
it came right down to making the tough choices necessary to bring that
change about, Marsha was just not able to do it. Of course, God is still
able to bring drastic healing in spite of our failures, and I pray that, in
His timing, He did just that.

HAVE A SEAT ON THE COUCH

1. In regard to parenting your defiant teen, do you sometimes feel that you keep doing the same things, the same way, expecting a different result? In what ways?

2. Do you, as a parent, have trouble "choosing your battles?" Why? And when you have chosen those battles, how critical do think it is to win that battle? Why?

3. How difficult is it for you to follow up on discipline decisions with your defiant child? Do you find it hard to always make sure that what you say will happen actually happens? Why or why not?

4. Are you a yeller? Were either of your parents yellers? Do you see yelling as a useful tool or a bad habit? Why? How does yelling make you feel? Does it help you communicate what you want it to communicate? Why or why not?

5. Do you feel as though you are giving your defiant child reason enough to change his or her behavior? Why or why not? What specific changes could you make right now to address this issue?

THAT KID MAKES ME SO MAD!

"That kid makes me so mad!" With these words, the mother of a defiant 15-year-old launched into a tale of frustration and woe. "She's just so unpleasant all the time. She battles us at every turn. She constantly argues about every little thing. She just never gives up. Always arguing, always saying hurtful things—and she does it just to get under our skin. And then when I get mad, I start yelling and using language that I'm not proud of. The other night, she yelled that she hated me, and before I could stop myself, I yelled, 'Well, I hate you too, you little %$#@!' I felt so bad afterward. But, man, that kid makes me so mad."

I've found that virtually every parent of a defiant teen is angry to some degree. For some, the anger comes out as irritation and confusion. Others struggle with guilt over what they acknowledge are harsh feelings toward their child. Many, however, are absolutely enraged. They harbor great resentment about the turmoil their teen has created in the home, and they have, in their hearts, all but given up hope of ever feeling love for the child again.

Although anger is an understandable response to dealing with a defiant teen, it inevitably leads to devastating consequences in the relationship. That's why later in this chapter, we'll develop a strategy for removing anger from your home and from your disciplinary approach with your defiant teen. But before we go there, I'd like to debunk a few myths about anger and show how this response to your child's behavior may be aggravating the problems in your home.

Nothing Makes You Mad

As a counselor, I have learned that what people say actually matters. The words we speak affect our outlook. If we say things that are untrue long enough, then we tend to start believing those untrue statements. For example, let's look again at how that exasperated mother began her conversation with me: "That kid makes me so mad!" Believe it or not, her statement was completely untrue. Yes, this mom may have been angry, but her daughter did not *make* her mad. Nothing *makes* us mad. We *choose* to respond with anger in certain situations.

I realize that I'm running the risk of being labeled a nitpicker, but I believe this distinction matters. If we continue to use the phrase, "[Fill in the blank] *makes* me mad," then we may start to believe that we are *forced* by other people or by circumstances to respond with anger. We begin to believe that we have no choice, no control over our response to a situation: "Those people or that circumstance *forced me to become angry against my will!*" And nothing could be further from the truth.

We are capable of emotional control. The writer of Proverbs declares, "Better a patient man than a warrior, a man who controls his temper than one who takes a city" (16:32). As we begin this examination of parental anger, it is crucial for us to understand that we have the capacity to have absolute, complete control over how we express our emotions. An angry response is not forced on us by anyone or anything; the choice of how to deal with a frustrating situation lies entirely with us.

So the obvious question arises, what would make us choose anger? I believe that parental anger stems from two sources: *what we believe* and *what our parents believed.*

The ABCs of Anger

I have found the work of Albert Ellis, founder of Rational Emotive Behavioral Therapy (REBT), a huge help as I assist kids and adults in determining the sources of some of their faulty thinking. REBT begins with the ABCs: *A* stands for the *activating event,* *B* stands for your *belief* about the activating event, while *C* stands for the *consequences* of the activating event. Now, before all that psychotherapeutic jargon prompts you to set this book on the nightstand and start counting sheep, let me walk you through a real-life scenario that helps explain the concept.

Bill and his wife had come to me seeking help for dealing with their overly rebellious 14-year-old son. Bill explained that he was completely out of patience: "Ryan came in last night and pushed my last button. I had all I was going to take of his smart mouth, so I warned him that he'd better shut up or he'd have to go to his room. When he didn't shut his mouth, I grabbed him by the arm to take him upstairs. That's when he took a swing at me and I had to defend myself by throwing him to the ground and holding him until he calmed down. Now, my wife will tell you that I had my hands around his throat at the time, but I don't remember it that way."

Although Bill's point was to demonstrate that his son was completely out of control, his description of this violent episode told me so much more about Bill than about his son. I was much more concerned with his behavioral choices than with Ryan's.

Here's how I walked him through the ABCs of emotional response: At the start of the scene Bill described, his son yelled at him and called him a name. That would be our *activating event*, or *A*. Bill responded by getting angry. This was the *consequence* of the activating event, or *C*. When I asked Bill why he was mad, he said, "I was mad at my son for speaking to me that way." Bill assumed that the activating event—Ryan's behavior—created the consequence of his anger. But here is what we know with absolute certainty: A*s never cause* C*s*. If *A*s cause *C*s, then all parents whose sons spoke to them in a disrespectful manner would respond in anger. To claim that the son's behavior *caused* the parent's response, we would have to confirm that anger is the universal response to disrespect across all peoples, all times and all cultures. And we know that this is definitely not the case. Many fathers would have responded to this exact scenario with calm resolve; others might have defused the situation with a lighthearted comment; and others may have been deeply saddened by the child's behavior. So anger is not a universal response to disrespectful words.

If *A*s don't cause *C*s, then what does? That's where *B* comes in. Your *belief* about the activating event is what causes the consequences. What Bill believed about his son's behavior determined his response, and the same is true for any parent. Exactly what you believe—and therefore your response to any given situation—can be influenced by several common sources of distorted thinking. Much of our anger stems from mental processes that are just not correct. These faulty mental processes are cognitive distortions—or, as I like to call them, *stinkin' thinkin'*.

Let's look briefly at some of the more common forms of stinkin' thinkin' that lead to a consequence of anger:

- **Catastrophizing.** This is when we view something as being more devastating than it actually is. In other words, we're making a mountain out of a molehill.

- **Black-and-white thinking.** This is the habit of viewing people or events as being either all good or all bad. The reality, of course, is that most are a combination of the two, but it's much easier to get mad at someone we perceive to be totally bad or in error.

- **Positive filtering.** When we block out anything that could be considered positive, we're left with nothing to focus on but the negatives of a situation.

- **Mindreading.** Parents get pulled into this all the time: assuming they know exactly what their child is thinking without having any hard evidence for it. They get all worked up over things the child may not actually be thinking at all.

- **Fortunetelling.** So often, people's perspectives are distorted by their confident predictions that negative things are going to happen. In reality, many of those dire events they foresee never actually happen.

These are just a few examples of how what you believe can lead to misplaced anger. When parents truly take the time to analyze the situation, they usually see that their faulty outlook—rather than their child's behavior—is what led to an angry response. By identifying your own tendencies toward stinkin' thinkin', you can learn to set aside those mistaken beliefs and choose to respond differently.

An Acorn Doesn't Fall Far from the Tree

I've mentioned before that what you saw modeled in your childhood home impacts your own parenting, but it bears repeating as we discuss the second source of parental anger. A small child is like a little video camera set to record 24/7. Monkey see, monkey do. We watched everything our parents did—and now our kids are watching everything we do, how we do it and why we do it. And how to control anger is one of the chief lessons we learn from childhood.

Whenever a couple comes into my office with concerns about a child's anger-control problem, I always ask which one of the parents has the anger-control problem. Inevitably, one or the other will acknowledge that, yes, they too sometimes struggle with expressing their anger appropriately. Then I ask which of *their* parents had the anger-control problem, and so on, and so on.

For the most part, how we manage our feelings of anger and frustration is a learned behavior. If you realize that you picked up some destructive anger habits from dear ol' dad, then it is your responsibility to break that cycle so that you don't pass the same harmful legacy on to your kids. It's time to halt this reincarnation of inappropriate irritation.

Ninety Percent of Parental Anger Is Sin

Based on the reactions I get from parents on a regular basis, I can almost hear you saying, "How can I *not* get angry when my kid acts this way?"

The truth is, we are going to get angry. You know it. I know it. And God knows it. Yet it seems pretty clear to me from reading Scripture that God does not delight in our anger. All the way back in the Old Testament, the Psalmist instructs us to "refrain from anger and turn from wrath" (37:8). And it seems as though every time Paul made a list of negative behaviors that believers should throw out like last week's trash, he made a point of including anger. For example, he exhorted the Ephesians to "get rid of all bitterness, rage and anger, brawling and slander, along with every form of malice" (4:31). And Colossians 3:8 commands, "But now you must rid yourselves of such things as these: anger, rage, malice, slander, and filthy language from your lips."

But since Jesus Himself got angry when He saw His Father's house being defiled (see John 2:13-22), we must conclude that anger in and of itself cannot be inherently sinful. Is it possible to be angry and not sin? Apparently so, because Paul instructed the people of the church in Ephesus, "In your anger, do not sin" (4:26). I guess we could say that anger is permissible when it is godly anger, a righteous indignation at the things that make God mad. All other expressions of anger seem to be forbidden. And since I don't see God getting mad at your defiant child just because she failed to obey you for the fifth time in five minutes, I would have to say that the vast majority of the anger expressed by parents is sinful.

Now, I can imagine you tensing up at my suggestion that you are sinning against God when you express anger toward your child. "You're asking the impossible! Anyone would get angry in my position. I wouldn't get so angry if my daughter wasn't completely obnoxious and defiant." That may be true, but her attitudes and behavior don't allow you to sidestep your responsibility before God. We are to parent our kids the way God parents us. I don't know about you, but I'm glad that I don't experience the wrath of God on a daily basis. If you want to relate to your child the way your heavenly Father relates to you, then your anger toward her must be curbed, if not eliminated altogether.

I can understand a parent being frustrated by a child's actions, disappointed by a child's decisions or even saddened by a child's attitude. But anger? Why? Why respond in anger? If your son brought home a failing grade in math, why get angry? Could it be that you believe his poor academic performance reflects badly on you and your family? If your daughter ignores your instructions multiple times, why get angry? Could it be that you believe she violated your "me time" and forced you to inconvenience yourself in order to deal with her misbehavior? Here's one I hear so often from kids: What if your son is not performing up to your standards out on the baseball field? Why, of all things would you respond with anger, as if his lack of hustle was as bad as coming up in the stands to kick dirt in your face? Could it be that, down deep, you believe that the other parents are judging you by your child's athletic prowess?

Maybe this sounds a bit harsh. After all, you're just a parent who is understandably passionate about teaching your children to always give their best effort as well as wanting them to grasp the importance of obeying those in authority. I understand, and I fully support those goals. But your passion has nothing to do with violating the clear instruction of Scripture by dumping anger on your child. There is no excuse for it. There is no "reason why."

It doesn't matter how rebellious or defiant your child may be; his behavior doesn't warrant an enraged response. Anger is one of the most devastating, destructive weapons a parent can wield. For this reason, every parent should be motivated to eliminate anger from interactions with their kids.

The Fatal Four

Parents tend to express anger in a variety of ways, any of which can be fatal to their efforts to reconnect with a defiant child and restore peace to the home. Let's look at four examples of how parents express sinful anger in devastating ways. Notice particularly how the message a parent intends to communicate through these behaviors becomes twisted and distorted.

Sarcasm

What a parent intends to communicate: "I am choosing humor rather than shouting to send a message that I don't like a particular behavior or situation."

What sarcasm actually communicates: "I feel contempt or condescension about the things that matter to you."

A 15-year-old girl stopped in the family room to say goodbye to her mom before heading out with her friends. In response to her daughter's inappropriate clothing, the mom said, "Wow! Look at you. Do you have your john meeting you at the motel, or are you going to just walk the streets till you pick one up? At least I hope you charge enough; those 'sexy' clothes have got to cost a pretty penny." (I'm not making this up, by the way. One of my clients described this actual encounter with her mother. No wonder the kid's in counseling.)

It's safe to say that this mother did not like the clothes that her daughter chose to wear. Your first thought, like mine, might be to wonder what those clothes were doing in the teenager's closet in the first place if mom didn't approve. But setting aside that conversation, let's consider the choices open to this mom when she saw how her daughter was dressed. She could . . .

A. Tell her politely to go back upstairs and put on more appropriate clothing.

B. Scream at her to get herself back upstairs and change unless she wants to be grounded for a month.

C. Attempt to use humor to lessen the possible tension of the situation.

D. Ignore it and keep on watching the Food Network.

She chose option C.

To her credit, she didn't scream, nor did she just give up and let the infraction go without comment. Instead, she tried to use humor and sarcasm to point out the problem. She may even have thought that her approach was more gentle than directly stating her contempt for her daughter's choice in evening attire. But sarcasm rarely softens the blow. Particularly in a home with a history of hurt feelings and frayed relationships, sarcasm is like a dagger thrust into the heart of a loved one.

Sarcasm can be understood as saying the opposite of what you really mean in an attempt at humor. However, it is a slippery two-way street. Between people with a very close bond, this sort of interaction can serve as a gesture of endearment. For example, just this Sunday I walked outside the main entrance of our church and approached a friend who was standing with a group of people near the door. "Hey, listen," I said. "I've been sent out here to ask you to move away from the door. We've had complaints that you're scaring away the guests."

We both laughed, and then he corrected me by saying, "No, it's not me. I heard it was your sermons that are scaring them off." Big laugh all around and everybody was having a good time. No harm; no foul. We were just good friends poking fun at each other.

Now let's say we repeat that scenario, but instead of approaching good friend, I walk up and say the exact same thing to a person who doesn't particularly like me and who suspects that I really don't like him. How do you think it would be taken? That's right—we'd probably end up in a fistfight in front of the worship center . . . a reassuring welcome for all our guests!

We need to understand that sarcasm can only cause more damage between people whose relationship is in some way strained. This means that sarcasm has no place in the home of an oppositional teen, where almost every relationship is stretched to the snapping point.

Yelling

What a parent intends to communicate: "I have reached my limit of patience and I am now taking control of the situation. I take this very seriously and I want you to know that I'm the one in power here."

What yelling actually communicates: "I am emotionally weak and vulnerable. I have no positive feelings toward you; in fact, at this moment I may hate, loathe and even reject you."

When it comes to accusations of sinning in anger toward our kids, most of us would have to plead "guilty" to the crime of yelling. Raising children is a stressful undertaking, even under the best of circumstances. All the responsibilities, the chores, the decisions and the organizational challenges place us under tremendous pressure, which builds and builds until we reach the limits of our capacity. Then, like spouting teakettles, we spew out steaming hot words, regardless of who might get burned.

I truly believe that when most parents raise their voice, they are trying to communicate the importance of the situation. They want their child to understand the seriousness of the events that are transpiring. They expect that when their child sees the veins bulging on their parent's forehead, notices the face slowly turning an alarming shade of violet and hears the thunderous volume of a voice raised in anger, they will realize that what they are doing is wrong and needs to come to a screeching halt. More often, however, rather than bringing the desired result, yelling serves only to sever the connection between parent and child. What a parent says in anger leaves a memory that can haunt a child for decades.

In times of anger, a person's brain is controlled more by adrenaline than by serotonin. In other words, angry brains don't function properly. This is why after an argument, you often feel compelled to apologize for something you said. If you had been "in your right mind" you never would have said those words.

One dad sat in my office racked with guilt. During an angry interchange, his daughter had screamed, "You're a #%$#@ loser! I wish you were dead!" And this father had replied, "Where was birth control when we really needed it?" Did he mean those words? No. Did he regret them? Yes. Will his daughter remember those cruel words for the rest of her life? Very likely.

In the midst of an anger-induced episode, we are not thinking correctly, so we let words slip out of our mouths that, under normal circumstances, would never cross our lips. When parents release their anger by yelling at their kids, they are not only in the wrong but they are in a prime position to be used of the Evil One to emotionally wound a child. This is why Scripture, from the Old Testament to the New, uniformly cautions us against being ruled by anger:

A fool shows his annoyance at once, but a prudent man overlooks an insult (Prov. 12:16).

A gentle answer turns away wrath, but a harsh word stirs up anger (Prov. 15:1).

Do not be quickly provoked in your spirit, for anger resides in the lap of fools (Eccles. 7:9).

My dear brothers take note of this: Everyone should be quick to listen, slow to speak and slow to become angry (Jas. 1:19).

Angry, vitriolic words hold the potential to devastate our children and to undermine our efforts to exert authority. As we observed in chapter 5, yelling shows not our strength but our emotional weakness. Anger-induced outbursts throw fuel on the fire of a defiant teen's own anger, so for a parent, they are a self-defeating strategy. In short, yelling yields no positive outcomes and brings a boatload of negatives.

Emotional Distancing

What a parent intends to communicate: "I am above the fray, demonstrating complete control over my emotions simply by remaining silent. By withdrawing, I expect to head off an angry interchange."

What emotional distancing actually communicates: "I reject your point of view and dismiss you as a person of value. I am punishing you by withholding love and affection."

Many times, getting away to cool down is not a bad idea. In fact, as we'll see a little later, this is one of the primary methods of avoiding more rancorous verbal exchanges. But emotional distancing involves more than taking a few minutes to pull yourself together; this term refers to withdrawing your affection, attention and positive regard from your child. We are talking here about the choice to clam up, go away, shut down, zone out or turn off communication when you feel offended by your child's words or actions.

This happens to be the area with which I struggle the most. When I get upset, I tend to shut down and clam up. While I think of myself as stoically avoiding a conflict, my wife says that I'm pouting like a three-year-old. I prefer my version.

I remember one specific evening when my son put in a disappointing performance at a football game. This was a rare event, since Josh was a successful athlete who nearly always played his hardest. But for whatever reason, things didn't go so well on this particular night. After I picked him up from the team's clubhouse, we rode home together in near silence, without our usual talk and banter about the game. The next day it dawned on me what I had done: Disappointed by the outcome of the game, a little upset at the ways things had turned out, I had shut down emotionally. I felt awful as I realized the message I had sent to my son through my emotional distancing: "If you don't perform up to my expectation, if you don't succeed in my eyes, then I will withdraw my love, affection and approval." Of course, I didn't consciously intend to communicate this damaging—and untrue—message, but that is exactly what I had done. I apologized to Josh for being such an emotional idiot and have since made a deliberate effort to notice early on when I fall into this pattern of response and then stop myself.

Dads tend to struggle with emotional distance more than moms do, for the same reasons that husbands tend to emotionally withdraw from their wives. Most men don't handle emotions very well. When in doubt, many of us just shut down and clam up. But recognizing the challenges the average guy faces because of his emotional make-up doesn't give us an excuse to behave in a way that damages our children. To shut down and emotionally withdraw doesn't win us brownie points for avoiding a conflict; this devastatingly selfish act can have long-lasting effects on our relationship with our kids, who need to know that we love them unconditionally and will never turn our backs on them.

Physical Aggression

What a parent intends to communicate: "I am in control and I will physically dominate you if that's what it takes to show you who's boss."

What physical aggression actually communicates: "I am out of control and just as emotionally immature as you. I believe that might makes right, and I'm no different than any bully you face at school."

Linda, a single mom, asked for my help in finding new ways to handle her defiant 14-year-old son, Robert. Having learned to yell from her own parents, she was quick to scream at Robert when his disobedience frustrated her. One of the first things we discussed was her need to put a lid on her own verbal outbursts. As Linda saw how this behavior on her part only reinforced her son's tendency to yell, she determined to correct this aspect of her parenting.

A few weeks after that breakthrough, she came into my office just bursting with eagerness to tell me about the changes that had taken place. "Robert is responding so well to me lowering my voice. I just can't believe it!" she enthused. "Just the other night, he was ignoring me when I asked him to do something. I just quietly got up, took his chin in my hand, looked him straight in the eye and said in a very calm voice, 'Robert, if you don't do exactly what I tell you, right this instant, I'm going to break every bone in your body.' And it was amazing, Jimmy. He did it!"

You can imagine what a proud moment it was for me as a counselor. I applauded Linda for learning to lower her voice, and then suggested we figure out a solution that didn't involve threats of criminal violence against her child.

Parents who resort to physical violence or the threat of physical violence as a way to demonstrate their parental authority and to motivate a child to comply are only proving their lack of parental authority. A characteristic problem among excessively defiant teens is the tendency to view their parents as peers rather than as elevated authority figures. This is why a 13-year-old daughter might call her mother a %$#@^ and why a 16-year-old boy might take a swing at his father when he feels that he's been wronged.

One of your most important tasks as the parent of a defiant teen is to communicate clearly and unmistakably to your child that you are not one of his peers. You are his parent—the primary authority figure in his life and the person who holds ultimate sway over every aspect of his existence.

Parents who do something as childish as physically striking a child are not only committing a crime, they are reinforcing by this adolescent behavior the idea that they are just another one of the teen's peers. Those who act like just another kid shouldn't be surprised when their children treat them like just another kid.

Before we move on from this topic, I should make clear that I am not talking here about never spanking a young child. I believe that spanking smaller children is not only permitted, but in some cases, it's the most appropriate discipline choice a parent can make. If a parent with a tiered discipline strategy has moved through all the other corrective options but a young child still chooses to disobey, then I believe that a firm swat on the backside is more than appropriate to make a parental point. But by the time a child reaches about 10 years of age, this physical deterrent should give way to more age-appropriate and, I believe, more effective means of motivation.

Kick the Anger Habit

All of these negative expressions of anger are simply bad habits parents fall into. Once these harmful patterns become your instinctive response, it takes a concerted effort to make the necessary changes and break these habits. But remember: You can't ask a teen to do something that you are not willing to do yourself. Most parents would be quick to punish a child who expresses anger with smart-mouth sarcasm or yelling or refusing to speak or physically striking out in anger. Yet how many parents act out in these ways every day? Curbing these negative behaviors in our own lives is essential if we ever want our kids to follow suit.

Here are some time-tested tips for breaking any bad habit:

- **Make a commitment to change, and then tell someone.** Any journey of change begins with a commitment. You have to have a specific destination in mind, as well as a sincere desire to get there. You also need to tell someone else about your plans. Choose a trusted friend who can pray for you and hold you accountable along the way.

- **Keep the commitment front and center.** Write down reminders of your commitment to change on note cards and post them in several places where you will see them multiple times during the day. You might tape a note to your bathroom mirror, place another on your nightstand, stick one on your dashboard and post one on your computer screen at work. Keeping the commitment front and center throughout the day will be a huge help in translating desire into action.

- **Determine alternative actions.** If you've made a commitment not to yell at your child when she disobeys, how *are* you going to respond? Predetermine your alternative plan of action. It's easier to avoid an old bad habit if the alternative behavior has been thought through and you are prepared to enact it.

- **If at first you don't succeed, try, try again.** Habits don't change overnight. If you have established a pattern of withdrawing emotionally during conflict, you will likely fail many times in your journey to success. This is to be expected. Rather than giving up in discouragement, seize each opportunity to recommit to change.

- **Pray and believe.** Seeking God's wisdom and guidance is an invaluable step in breaking these negative habits. You can be assured, without a shadow of doubt, that it is God's will that you rid your life of any and all of these negative expressions of anger. If you ask, He will give you the strength and the stamina necessary to follow His will.

Removing Anger from the Discipline Process

I hope you can see now that it is absolutely vital for us to deal with our own anger issues before attempting to deal with the anger issues in our defiant kids. As parents, we set the emotional tone, the example and the stage for the eventual removal of all out-of-control anger episodes from the home.

When our kids do something wrong, most of us are quick to think about how to make this situation a teachable moment for our child. We want God to use this incident as a tool to sculpt them ever closer to the image of His Son. But these discipline episodes, so fraught with potential for anger and tension, are also teachable moments for us. I believe that our heavenly Father is just as interested in how *we* handle these tenuous situations as in how our children respond to them. Our task is to remain open to His Spirit and His prompting during stressful discipline episodes, so that we too will be molded into the image of Christ. We must remember, as we try to teach and instruct our children, that our Father is still attempting to teach and instruct us.

That leaves us with the question, what can parents do to remove anger from the discipline process? Have you ever been a part of a business deal or a work situation in which some of the involved parties got a tad tense? During times like this, chances are good that someone said something like, "Hey, this isn't personal. It's just business." Well, that is exactly the attitude that works best when disciplining oppositional kids. Your personal mantra should be, *I'm not angry. I'm not disappointed. I'm not frustrated. The discipline decision I'm about to deliver is not personal; it's just business.* A dispassionate attitude during the discipline process is, I believe, like Willie Wonka's Golden Ticket for parents of defiant children: It's your pass into a wonderland that, instead of chocolate, flows with sweet calm and peace. So how do you develop and maintain this dispassionate attitude? Let me give you three rules for removing anger from the discipline process.

Rule 1: Remember that Your First Response Is Your Worst Response

Back in the mid-'90s, Beth and I went to Dallas for a weekend conference, leaving our adolescent kids in the care of various families of friends. After a great weekend, we were making the three-hour trek back to Austin when I got a call on my cell. Apparently, one of my wonderful, darling, angelic children had made a colossally bad decision while we were gone, had gotten caught, and was now calling to inform us of the mishap rather than waiting until we got home to smack us in the kisser with the whole situation.

I mentioned earlier that I tend to become emotionally distant when I get angry. But not this time. You might say that I was extremely involved, emotionally speaking! With anger seething through my brain, all I could think about for next hour of the trip was how to convince Child Protective Services that strangulation was not necessarily child abuse. When Beth assured me she had no intention of bailing me out of jail, I considered other possible discipline scenarios, from grounding for life to forcibly enrolling my sweet child in a cloistered convent. By the time we were passing through Waco, about halfway home, I had determined that she would be grounded for at least a couple of months, would not be permitted to drive until I felt good and ready to give back the keys, and would not be allowed to associate with certain friends until Jesus gloriously returned to split the eastern sky.

But as we reached the outskirts of Austin, I began to realize that my initial reaction was primarily adrenaline-driven, not Jesus-driven. My first thoughts had been based more on hurt feelings and pent-up anger than on what was best for my child or on how God desired to bring good out of this situation. By the time we pulled into the driveway, the Holy Spirit had cooled my emotions, and my heavenly Father had reminded me of the many times I had fallen and He had picked me back up. So when the front door opened and I saw the look of anguish on my little girl's face, all I could do was hug that baby for all she was worth. Was she punished for her choices? Oh, yeah. But God redeemed that negative experience and morphed it into a positive event in the life of my daughter and my family. She learned a valuable lesson that fateful day, and so did I: My *first* response is my *worst* response.

When a child does something that requires discipline, those are often tense moments, full of anxiety, frustration and anger. When we face an anxiety-producing situation like that, our bodies respond by ramping up for the battle. This is commonly known as the "fight or flight" response. But as we saw earlier, when our adrenaline is pumping and our blood pressure is soaring, we are not primed to make rational, level-headed decisions. Instead, our minds race to extremes, reflecting the extreme nature of our emotional condition.

One father told me that his son was caught vandalizing cars, but the neighbor chose not to call the police. In a rage, this father declared that, since vandalism was a criminal offense that would have resulted in the boy going to prison until age 18, had he been arrested, his consequence was to be grounded until his eighteenth birthday. At the time, the boy was 14 years old.

Making rash proclamations in the heat of the moment is detrimental for two reasons. First, a discipline decision born of passion rather than a desire for redemption is usually overly severe, not appropriate to the crime committed. Thus, it will affirm your child's belief that you are uncaring and unfair. Second, when you make dramatic promises or overly harsh threats that you'll never keep, you lose credibility with your kids. (When our junior-high-age daughter was acting up at the mall one day, Beth threatened, "If you don't stop, I'll never take you shopping again!" Oh, how I wish that edict could have come true.)

Remember: When a discipline crisis hits, the first rule for removing anger from the equation is to resist the temptation to go with your initial response.

Rule 2: Bring God into the Situation ASAP

In the midst of a disciplinary conflict with your child, the last thing you want to do is handle it on your own. Instead, your best strategy is to get out of the way and let Jesus flow through you to handle the situation. This is exactly the thought behind Paul's words in Galatians 2:20: "It is no longer I who live, but Christ lives in me" (*NASB*). Your response will be much more successful and less prone to mistakes if you bring God into the discipline process at the earliest possible moment, echoing the word of John the Baptist when he said of Jesus, "He must become greater; I must become less" (John 3:30).

With that in mind, let me walk you through four steps to calling a S.T.O.P. to an anger-filled discipline episode.

Stop and Separate

This step is a response to the knowledge that your first response is your worst response. Your first instinct in the midst of an angry, emotional exchange with a defiant teen may be to argue with her, lecture her or proclaim an immediate discipline decision. All of these will just make a bad situation intolerable, so you need to create time and space to calm down. Separate yourself from the offending child until your adrenaline rush, and hers, subside.

This may be difficult when tempers are flaring, but it is essential. I propose using the phrase, "I'm calling a stop to this" as a way of signaling that tempers are elevating and that a period of separation is needed. If the child refuses, then additional disciplinary actions will be warranted, but by using that catch phrase, you can alert all parties involved to the need to calm down. And anyone can use the phrase—you, your child, your spouse. Anyone who feels that things are escalating out of control can call for a break, during which everyone goes to separate rooms and allows their temper to settle down before the discipline discussion moves forward.

Of course, if you just separate and never come back to the issue, that's called *avoidance*, which is a very unhealthy way of dealing with stressful issues. So limit your stop-and-separate period to no more than 30 to 60 minutes. Then come back together to resume the discussion of the issue.

Tone Down the Tension

During your separation break, you need to focus on letting the anger out and getting a realistic perspective on the situation. This is the time for you and your spouse to discuss the issue. Or if you're alone with your teen, call your spouse or seek the counsel of other family or friends. If the anger persists and you just can't seem to calm down, try to "change the channel of your brain" by watching TV or doing some yard work. Do whatever it takes to focus your mind on something other than your intense feelings or anger toward your child.

Open Your Heart to God

This is done, of course, through prayer. Pray that God will give you the ability to overcome your feelings of anger. Pray that this event will be a teachable moment for both you and your child. Pray for the wisdom and grace to approach your child with the heart of Christ, not a heart filled with rage or vengeance. And claim the promise from Luke 12:12, in which Jesus instructed His disciples not to worry when they were dragged before any city officials or religious authorities because "the Holy Spirit will teach you at that time what you should say."

In the same way, the Holy Spirit will guide you as you speak to your defiant teen in the midst of a discipline episode. If you pray that God will use your voice to communicate His will to your child, don't worry about what to say. The Holy Spirit will give you the perfect words to use at the right time. That's a promise. After you spend a few minutes seeking the Father's face, you'll find anger no longer has much power over you.

Present Christ to Your Child

God desires more than anything else to be reconciled with your rebellious teenager. He loves that child beyond your ability to comprehend and wants to be reunited in a close, personal, intimate relationship. You are an instrument in His hands to accomplish that desire.

Paul said it best in 2 Corinthians 5:20: "We are therefore Christ's ambassadors, as though God were making his appeal through us. We implore you on Christ's behalf: Be reconciled to God." What is an ambassador? It is a nation's representative on foreign soil. That is exactly what you are! When you re-enter the room to talk with your defiant child, you are Christ's representative in that conversation. This knowledge should make a profound difference in how you approach these situations. This discipline event is not about you lowering the boom or making your child regret ever messing with you. It's about your heavenly Father desiring reconciliation with your child and your being His representative in that room to help bring that about.

Remember that S.T.O.P. is a strategy to bring God into the discipline process, but it can be used in any tension-filled parent-child situation, even outside of a disciplinary conflict. The most important aspect of S.T.O.P is ensuring that both parties—parent and child—drop the argument and separate. The rest of the process cannot work if the argument is carried on uninterrupted, all over the house.

Rule 3: See Discipline as Redemptive, Not Punitive

We've touched on this before, but it's such an important truth that it warrants its own rule. This is a fundamental change in the way most of us view our role in discipline. We learned from a young age that the fear of punishment is the motivating force behind all discipline. This may be true from a child's perspective, but we parents have to aim higher than that.

Just this week, one of my clients, a single mom, did such a great job with her two very defiant teenagers and provided a perfect example of what we're talking about. Both kids were acting up at a restaurant, and when their mom attempted to correct them, they responded with disrespect. When they all got back in the car, she told the two teens that their behavior was not acceptable and they could expect several specific consequences to be enforced during the coming week. Needless to say, both kids were beside themselves with anger, disgust and disbelief that their lame mother would respond like this. When the family arrived home, the two teenagers were instructed to go to their own rooms.

Many parents would have just dropped the issue, grateful to go on about their busy day. Not this mom. About an hour later, she went up to see her son. They had a terrific conversation, tears were shed and she could sense that redemption was present in the room.

Then she went to her daughter's room, where she was rebuffed at the door. Yet this determined mom forged ahead and sat next to her daughter on the bed to explain the situation. She tried to paint a picture of why she had made her decision and of how much she loved this girl and her brother, more than either of them could know. Even though this very angry young lady refused to allow even a glimmer of kindness to show through her cloak of fury, this mom took courage in knowing that she'd spoken the words her kids needed to hear and set forth the discipline her kids needed to experience—the rest was up to God.

What I love about this mom is that she didn't stop at punishment; her focus all along was redemption—and God will honor that commitment.

To Sum It Up

In this chapter, we learned that nothing—not our kids, not our circumstances—has the power to *make* us mad. When we respond with anger, it's a choice that has more to do with our faulty thinking and with the way we were raised than with anything our kids have done. In addition, 90 percent of all parental anger is sinful, a destructive tool of the Enemy to damage the parent-child relationship.

We looked at the fatal four negative expressions of anger—sarcasm, yelling, emotional distancing and physical aggression—and compared what parents intend to communicate through these behaviors with the message their teens actually receive. This led to the conclusion that, given the destructive impact of out-of-control anger, the only solution is to kick the anger habit. Parents can accomplish this by following some key steps for breaking bad habits and by observing three rules for removing anger from the discipline process:

- Rule 1: Remember that your *first* response is your *worst* response.
- Rule 2: Bring God into the situation ASAP.
- Rule 3: See discipline as redemptive, not punitive.

A Quick Follow-up

You'll recall Linda, who was so proud of her son's response to her lowered voice during a conflict. Yes, she did lower her voice, but then she calmly threatened her son, Robert, with physical violence. Now, Robert was a very difficult case. He was diagnosed with bipolar disorder and had many more anger outbursts before he was properly medicated. The family rules had to be clearly explained several times before they were understood, and then underscored with a behavior contract. Even though Linda's yelling was a learned behavior from her childhood, she worked very hard to eliminate this harmful habit from her interactions with her son. Though she had slip-ups from time to time, overall she was able to defeat the habit and relate to Robert in a much more calm, understanding and controlled way. When I finished seeing them, their situation had very much improved.

HAVE A SEAT ON THE COUCH

1. Would you say that you struggle with anger as the parent of a defi-ant child? If so, what form does your anger tend to take—sarcasm, yelling, emotional distancing or physical aggression?

2. Looking back at the types of faulty thinking that spark so much of the anger that parents feel, which cognitive distortion do you strug-gle with? How does this stinkin' thinkin' affect your parenting?

3. Which of the fatal four displays of anger do you most often strug-gle with? How did you feel when reading about what this action ac-tually communicates to your teen?

4. How hard do you feel it will be to kick the habit of using these neg-ative anger expressions? What are some alternative actions you could take?

5. When you look at the three rules for removing anger from the dis-cipline process, do they seem practical, or did you dismiss them as blah-blah-blah psychobabble? What do you anticipate will be your biggest obstacle in following these rules in your home?

7

YOUR SECRET WEAPON

What I'm about to share with you is, in my opinion, the most powerful tool available to parents of extremely defiant kids. I have seen this instrument help change the living environments of countless families. It helps the kids, it helps the parents and it helps the parents' marriage. This tool is relatively easy to develop and more or less trouble-free in its implementation.

What is this miracle of superior parenting? A behavior contract.

I can almost hear your sigh of disappointment from where I sit. You appear to be somewhat underwhelmed by my unique and ingenious choice of strategy. If we were meeting over coffee, you'd probably grumble, "This is like telling me that the new, revolutionary method of fixing my car is to take it to a mechanic! Wow, Myers, I'm bowled over by the sheer magnitude of your genius!"

Okay, so a behavior contract is not exactly a new idea. Nor is it all that unique or ingenious. In fact, I wouldn't be surprised to hear that you've tried to implement one of these in your home before without much success. So why am I making such a big deal about an old parenting horse that's been ridden too many time? Because everything I said in the first paragraph is true. I do believe that a behavior contract is the best weapon a parent has for winning the struggle with an extremely defiant child. And I have seen it change the lives of kids, couples and entire families.

The problem is not that contracts don't work; it's that, more often than not, we don't properly work the contract. So even if you've tried a contract in the past, hang with me here. I'm asking you to give the old nag one more opportunity to show you what she's got.

What Is a Behavior Contract?

If you don't already know what a behavior contract is and were kind enough not to belittle me at the start of this chapter, here's a quick overview: A behavior contract has two parts. First, it clearly states the parents' expectations for the defiant child. It clearly defines, in writing, the behavioral boundaries of the family, both at home and away. Now, if this was all that a behavior contract involved, then it would just be a glorified list of house rules, but a behavior contract takes a critical next step: It also clearly states the exact consequences that will be administered if a boundary is violated. In sum, a behavior contract is a clearly defined list of expectations with clearly defined consequences for violating those expectations clearly listed right alongside them.

You may have noticed my gratuitous use of the word "clearly." No, it's not that I couldn't come up with another adjective. I simply want to emphasize that setting *clear* parental intentions is the main purpose behind using a contract. Doing so reduces, if not eliminates, ambiguity in the discipline process. Parents know exactly what the rules are and exactly what the consequences for breaking those rules will be, and the kids know exactly the same thing. This approach eliminates guesswork, averts hastily decided attempts at fair and balanced discipline and prevents inconsistency in applying consequences from one incident to another.

As a parent under stress, it can be difficult to remember exactly what you decided the last time your kid misbehaved. It's even harder to be aware of a past discipline decision your spouse made. But you can be sure your child remembers. Exceptionally defiant teens tend to be remarkably legalistic. They're looking to escape the consequences of their decisions by any means necessary, so they'll grasp at the slightest technicality they think might get them off the hook. One young man sat in my office as we discussed his decision to have sex with his girlfriend. With a look of creative achievement on his face, he proclaimed, "But I was wearing a condom, so I didn't *technically* touch her!" He thought that he had discovered the long desired "get out of jail free" card for sexual impurity. He was so proud that he had figured out a way to outsmart the rules.

He and his cohort of defiant teens are looking for every loophole and seeming contradiction that might help them circumvent parental authority. Your child will scrutinize each disciplinary verdict for the slightest inconsistency in order to throw that inconsistency in your face as an example of your inept parenting ability.

For this reason alone, a contract is the best tool I know for eliminating discipline ambiguity by making inarguably clear what is expected of your teen and laying out specific consequences for violating those expectations.

Five Benefits of a Behavior Contract

Remember those old western movies where a wagon would pull into a dusty old town and the driver would fold down a platform, then put up a big sign that read something like "Doc Martin's Magic Metabolic Snake Oil Elixir"? The barker would rally the townspeople by promoting the miraculous properties of a tonic that could cure everything from chigger bites and liver disease to menopause, gout and hoof-and-mouth disease. This concoction held the cure for whatever ailed you. In an odd way, that's how I feel about the usefulness of a behavior contract—and unlike snake oil, I believe it works. It addresses nearly all of the most prominent problems created by a defiant child. In fact, I'd like to tell you about the five biggest advantages of using a behavior contract. So step right up, friends and neighbors, and witness this miracle for yourselves.

1. It Changes the Discipline Dynamic

During the discipline process, the sides are unmistakably drawn. In the red corner weighing in at . . . well, let's just skip that part . . . we have the Parent, also known as . . . the Punisher! And in the black corner, weighing in at a whopping 97 pounds, we have the Child, also known as the Punishee. Everyone knows that a parent's job as the Punisher is to "bring the heat" and make sure that the kid learns a valuable lesson from the pain. It is also universally known that the Punishee's job is to whine, complain and throw a fit to resist said "heat." But what if this well-worn dynamic could be changed? What if, as the Parent, you didn't have to be portrayed as the bad guy all the time?

A behavior contract can do just that. Once the contract is in place and the rules and consequences are clear to everyone in the house, you can move toward an old-English style of law and order. Do you remember from high school history the Latin phrase *Lex Rex*? It means "the Law is King." Not *Rex Lex*. The king isn't the law; the rules don't depend on who happens to be on the throne. In a similar way, our homes need to operate on a *Lex Rex* system of government, where the Law is King no matter which parent happens to be home. When the contract is implemented, *it* becomes the law. It, not you, becomes the Punisher. When the agreed-upon contract is violated, then the agreed-upon consequences laid out in the contract are enacted. When a child knows where the boundaries lie and chooses to violate them, then he chooses to accept the consequences. You, as the parent, have little to do with it.

This reminds me of the discipline style taught in the *Jerry Maguire* School of Parenting. Do you remember that movie? Playing in the title role, Tom Cruise is a high-powered sports agent whose star NFL client was played by Cuba Gooding, Jr. In one scene in which he tries to make the player understand his role as the agent, Maguire pleads, "Help me help you! Help *me* . . . help *you*!" This can be your stance with a defiant child: "Help me help you." Your child needs to understand that if she keeps up her present negative behavior, the contract is going to kick in and then there's no way to switch it off. As the loving parent, you're trying to help your child avoid this ugly scenario. The interchange could go something like this: "Hey, sweetheart, you're getting a little ramped up here. You know that you'll lose all your electronics for a week if you act disrespectfully to me. You don't want that to happen and I don't want that to happen, so let's take a break to calm down so you don't have to deal with the consequences of the contract."

A contract can dramatically change the discipline dynamic in the home.

2. It Helps Parents Stay on the Same Page

One of the biggest negatives of raising a defiant child is that, in many cases, discipline becomes a divisive issue for the parents. As we have mentioned earlier, many times the husband looks at discipline differently than his wife does. And this dissension in the ranks is like blood in the water to an extremely defiant child. As we discussed previously, standing together, agreeing on a unified course of action and presenting a united front against an opponent who is actively seeking an opening for attack is essential to successfully parenting a defiant child. A contract is enormously helpful in this regard.

In the early stages of developing a contract, I suggest that each spouse formulate their own list of rules and identify consequences they think should go with each rule. Once those initial lists are complete, the husband and wife then merge their individual ideas into one unified contract. Since this will be especially tricky for spouses who don't agree on their discipline approach, I suggest the parents find an hour or two when they can be alone. I know that in a hectic family this can be difficult, but desperate times require desperate measures.

Landing on a mutually satisfying contract will require good-willed negotiation on the part of each spouse. The stricter spouse will have to agree to a discipline strategy that may be more lenient than he or she would like, and the more lenient spouse will have to agree to a discipline strategy that may be stricter than he or she would like. Remember that in a good negotiation, no one gets *everything* they want but everyone gets *something* they want. A spouse who feels bullied into something will be less likely to enforce the contract once in place, so make sure that each spouse truly agrees with the boundaries and the consequences before finalizing the contract.

Once you have successfully negotiated a final behavior contract, you both have to commit to enforcing it regardless of how you may feel about the particular rule violated or the consequences to be imposed. If both parents are not fully committed to enforcing the contract, there is no way on earth you can expect your child to adhere to it. A contract provides the perfect opportunity for parents to put away their petty parenting differences for the sake of their child. Always keep in mind that being unified as a parenting team will have an astronomically greater impact on the welfare of your child than any particular rule infraction.

3. It Reduces Parental Stress

Foreknowledge is a beautiful thing. Take TiVo and the Dallas Cowboys for example. I have not missed a Cowboys game since I was in elementary school in the 1960s. Sitting at my father's knee, I learned to cuss and throw things at the TV whenever the Boys didn't play well. And thanks to modern technology, I'm certain never to miss a game in the future. If I have a scheduling conflict, I simply TiVo the game so that I can watch it later.

Sometimes, however, I inadvertently learn the final score before I get a chance to watch the game. Has this ever happened to you? It takes all the fun—all the excitement, suspense and anxiety—out of the game because I already know what's going to happen.

Knowing exactly what the consequences will be *before* a boundary is violated accomplishes the same thing. It takes all the anxiety and uncertainty away because the contract has already determined the required course of action.

Coming up with creative, fair, equitable and just consequences during the heat of conflict can be extremely nerve-racking. *What do I do? When do I do it? Would my spouse agree with this decision? What did I do that last time this happened?* All of these questions and more race through the mind of a parent when an infraction is first discovered. Making the right call in the midst of conflict is a daunting task.

When I was a youth minister, we had what we called a "rule infraction policy" in place during every trip that we took with the youth of the church. This policy highlighted three rules that, if violated, would result in a student being sent home at the parent's expense, no questions asked. The parents of each youth signed this policy, as did each kid who went on a trip. These were the rules:

1. You may not enter the room of a member of the opposite sex without the approval and presence of an adult sponsor.

2. You may not use or be in possession of any illegal substance.

3. You may not demonstrate repeated disrespect for adult authority.

If a youth was found to be in violation of any of these three rules, it was time to say goodbye. There was no discussion and no handwringing over to what to do. It was a straightforward matter of a direct phone call: "Hello, Mom and Dad? Come pick me up. I'm a-comin' home." That predetermined discipline decision alleviated an enormous amount of stress for the adults on those trips. Again, the sponsoring adults were not the bad guys. The kids and parents had each signed the policy and knew what would happen if they violated them. A student who chose to violate the rule also chose to receive the consequences; it was not a matter of the sponsors being mean or unfair.

A contract can alleviate the same kind of parental stress in the home. And if you're living with a defiant teen, you need all the stress-reducers you can get.

4. It Eliminates Inconsistency

Okay, this is a big one. More often than anything else, parents who come to my office cite inconsistency as their worst parenting mistake. They simply don't follow through with what they say they will do. Grounding the child for a week seemed like a good idea at the time, but upon further review, Mom realizes that she'll be more inconvenienced by that consequence than her child will be, so she lets the defiant teen off after two days. Or parents take away their son's television privileges for the rest of the day, then later find him sprawled on the couch watching his favorite show; things have calmed down and they don't want to risk another blowup, so they just let it slide.

A contract can help parents be consistent with their discipline decisions. Since the discipline choices are no longer arbitrary but predetermined by the contract, the parents have a better chance of following through. Something about putting the terms in writing gives a sense of permanence to it. Having the specific consequences attached to specific offenses posted on the refrigerator holds the parent accountable to follow through with what is posted. A contract puts the parent's credibility on the line. Your word is now written in black and white for all the world to see. Do you mean what you say? Will you do what you've said you will do? Many times having a written contract is just the motivation a battle-fatigued parent needs to follow through with discipline decisions.

5. It Protects the Teen from Excessive Discipline

Yes, a contract is a wonderful tool to help parents enforce consistent boundaries with a defiant child, but it can be a lifesaver for the child as well. As we've seen, our first response is our worst response. Most parents tend to get angry in the heat of conflict, and most of us would confess to punishing our kids in anger from time to time . . . or almost all the time. This means that most of us also have had the experience of punishing our kids excessively, to our later regret. Excessive discipline results when a parent—without much forethought and in a fog of fatigue, frustration, exasperation and anger—delivers a punishment that far outweighs the crime committed.

The formula goes something like this:

Fatigue + Frustration + Exasperation + Anger = Excessive Discipline

None of us deliberately sets out to overreact; we just sort of erupt into excessive discipline. For example, a 16-year-old boy came home 30 minutes past his curfew for the second time that school year. His mother, who had missed three days of work because of the flu, felt horrible. She didn't have the energy to deal with her son's disobedience right then, but she remembered warning him at his first curfew offense that he'd be in big trouble if it ever happened again. It angered her even more that he pulled a stunt like this while she was feeling so bad. Under the influence of the flu and outraged by her child's lack of respect for her authority, she started shouting herself hoarse before he even made it into the living room. "That's it, young man. I've had it with you! You have ignored me for the last time, and you, my friend, are grounded for the next three months!"

Obviously, this mother was frustrated and exhausted, and certainly the child deserved to suffer some consequences for his actions. But three months? Here's where a contract could save both the child and the mother a lot of grief. If the contract clearly states that he will be grounded for one week for missing curfew, then all that's left is for both parties to hold to their agreement. No fuss, no shouting, no cries of injustice.

One other note here: Sometimes, in the heat of anger, parents will punish a child beyond what the contract states. When the child points this out, the parent will say something like, "Listen, I'm the parent here. I don't have to abide by any piece of paper. I do whatever I want!" While I understand the concept of sovereignty and authority, you cannot ask your child to abide by a contractual agreement if you are not willing to abide by it yourself. It is critically important for your own integrity and for the future success of this discipline strategy that you stick to the contract—just as you are asking your child to follow it.

Constructing a Successful Behavior Contract

Now that we've seen all the benefits of a behavior contract, let's look at exactly what it takes to put such a contract into place. Of course, a major portion of any contract is the stipulation of consequences for violating the terms of the agreement. This is such a vital component that we will devote the entire next chapter to crafting effective consequences. For now, we'll touch on the idea of consequences only briefly as part of the overall plan for creating a winning behavior contract.

Set Realistic Expectations and Reasonable Consequences

Realistic expectations and reasonable consequences are absolutely essential to an effective contract. Setting unrealistic standards that require a child to achieve perfection only assures defeat. If the speed limit on every American highway was 10 MPH, we would have to increase our law enforcement personnel a thousand fold to just to write all the speeding tickets required. The highways would be shut down by traffic jams because so many cars would be pulled over. If the rules of the highway are too strict, then the transportation system won't work the way it was designed. The same is true of our homes. If the rules are excessively strict, then our families simply won't work the way they were designed.

Requiring straight *As* in all honors courses or setting a bedtime of 8 PM for a 17-year-old will lead to frustration and conflict with most children. As a general rule, I advise parents to stay within the expectations of normal Christian households. You don't want to be too strict or too lenient. You must have a basis from which to assure your defiant child that you aren't "crazy" and that your rules are not "wack." You want to be able to say that your rules are, in fact, within the norms for most Christian families.

Avoiding overly harsh consequences in your contract is also important. If you are always grounding your child for six months at a time, then the odds of those consequences actually being enforced are slim to none. Consequences must be set at a reasonable level so that you, as the parent, can assure they will be carried out. As we've discussed, failing to carry out the consequences destroys the effectiveness of the contract.

Specify Areas of Expectation

Because you aren't concerned only with your child's behavior at home but also have expectations for his or her behavior elsewhere, you'll want to create a fairly comprehensive contract. You need to make your expectations clear in the following areas:

- **Home conduct.** What specific behaviors are expected and which behaviors are not acceptable in your home? How do you expect your child to treat other family members? What particular activities within the home will be governed by this contract?

- **Home chores.** And I really hope your child has some. Helping out around the house is a vital teaching tool to show how everyone in the family pitches in to help make the home function. This expectation goes a long way in combating a child's exaggerated sense of entitlement.

- **School conduct.** What behaviors do you specifically expect of your children while at school? They need to realize that, as representatives of your family, their behavior at school is important to you as a parent. If they choose to misbehave there, they will pay the price at home.

- **School grades.** What specific goals or standards will you set for your child's academic performance? Keep in mind that there is a difference between a substandard grade with effort and a substandard grade due to lack of effort.

- **Community conduct.** What are your expectations for your child's behavior within the community as a whole? What are the consequences for a speeding ticket or being found in possession of a controlled substance? Yes, such offenses bring legal consequences, but they should have family ramifications as well.

- **Problem behaviors.** What behaviors have created the most conflict or provoked the most discipline issues over the past few months? Whatever those infractions may be, make sure to specifically reference them in the contract. This will ensure that current problem behaviors are individually singled out to prevent any ambiguity.

Determine Your "School Zone"

Most communities have set aside school zones for the purpose of creating safe places for their children. They vigorously discourage motorists from speeding in a these zones. And by what means to they discourage speeding? Dollars and cents. In fact, not that many cents are involved—penalties primarily consist of lots and lots of dollars. Most towns have made exceeding the speed limit in a school zone such a huge financial hardship that drivers tend to get whiplash from braking so abruptly before they enter the area.

Certainly, cities punish speeding on all roadways, but they set severe financial penalties for speeding in a school zone. Why? To reduce that problem to its lowest possible level.

You can put this same principle to work in your home by determining your "school zones." Let's say that your defiant child's biggest problem is acting disrespectfully to you and other authority figures. If that's the case, then disrespectful behaviors should receive the harshest consequence. If your child struggles with disobedience, then that behavior should be met with the most severe penalties. Obviously, you will determine consequences for all inappropriate behavior, but you'll target the most egregious behavior with the most painful of penalties in order to reduce that problem to its lowest possible level.

Simplify Consequences

We'll spend the entire next chapter considering the issue of consequences, but for now I'd like you to keep in mind that virtually all infractions a child commits in the home can be grouped into three categories: disrespect, disobedience and dishonesty. Instead of cluttering your contract with lots of separate consequences for lots of separate offenses, you can identify specific consequences for each category: one for disrespect, one for disobedience and one for dishonesty.

For example, if your defiant child uses profanity and doing so is against house rules, he would suffer the consequences for disobedience. If the child storms out of a room and slams a door, that would be disrespectful, so the consequences for disrespect would be applied. This simplified strategy also allows for a tiered approach. If a child, for example, steals something from her mother's purse, lies about it and then acts disrespectfully when caught, all three consequences could be added together to match the severity of the multiple offenses.

Insert an Attitude Addendum

What happens if your defiant child gets mad and starts yelling while you are trying to communicate the consequences for, let's say, losing his temper in an angry outburst? That's where an attitude addendum comes in handy. The contract should stipulate that if the child chooses to be disrespectful during the implementation of the contract, then the consequences he would have experienced for his offense will be doubled.

Keep in mind that, after your child violates the contract, you'll want to have a cooling down period for all parties so that the adrenaline can subside before you have the conversation about consequences. But if the child still wants to get ramped up, then you can ask quietly ask him to reconsider this behavior to avoid doubling the consequences already earned. Remind your child that he doesn't have to like the consequence assigned by the contract, but he must treat you with respect.

Include the Whole Family

To avoid singling out a defiant child as the official "black sheep" of the family, make the contract apply to all the children in the house. You may have to tweak the consequences to be more age-appropriate or to stipulate different rules that are more inclusive, but identifying it as a family contract, like a spoonful full of sugar, helps the medicine go down. Some parents even include consequences to address their own problem behaviors, such as raising their voice or using profanity. For example, the parent can pay a dollar into a jar per offense, then take the kids out for ice cream with the proceeds.

Keep the Door Open to Change

Somewhere within the body of the contract, you'll want to specify that these expectations and consequences are simply a starting point. Rules will be added or subtracted and consequences will be adjusted on a regular basis.

For instance, if the consequences set forth in the contract don't provide sufficient motivation for change, then they will be increased as needed. If a consequence of three days without electronics does not motivate your child to stop acting disrespectfully to a parent, then the contract will increase the consequence to five days. Of course, the child will not be held accountable for any change until it is placed in the contract and discussed.

Start with All or Nothing

Contracts are sometimes initiated during times of relative calm when the child isn't already under a disciplinary consequence. Other times, a contract is put in place during an exceptionally difficult period, when the child has already lost most of his privileges. Depending on the current situation, you can choose to begin the contract with all privileges granted or all privileges removed. For example, if everything is relatively calm when the contract is instituted and the child has most, if not all, of his privileges in place, then the contract begins from a standpoint of having privileges removed as a consequence for negative behavior. But if most or all of the child's privileges have already been removed, then the contract could be the means by which he earns those privileges back through good behavior.

These suggestions are intended as helpful hints for creating a successful behavior contract for an exceptionally defiant child. The process of creating an effective contract for your home will undoubtedly be an exercise in trial and error. You will learn from your first draft things that some things work and others need to be adjusted for your family. But if you hang in there, in time you will have a written behavioral contract that will go a long way in reducing the anger and tension in your home.

Of course, creating a contract is only a small part of the battle. Implementation is the key to making it all work.

Making a Contract Work

I grew up in Cisco, a small town that sits right on the edge of where north-central Texas gives way to the rolling plains of the West. When I lived there, we played 2A football. We had our hands full playing against all the other small towns in the area, but one year we actually scrimmaged the team from the big city of Brownwood, at the time a 4A school. We only played against their JV squad, but those of us on the Cisco team were convinced we had reached the big show! I guess our coach could tell we were slightly intimidated as we pulled up and looked out the bus windows at these guys, who all stood over seven feet tall and weighed at least 300 pounds. I remember him looking at us and saying, "Boys, they put on their pants on one leg at a time, just like you do."

Someone in the back of the bus said, "Yeah, Coach, but their pants are so much bigger than ours!"

The coach replied, "You know, on paper they are bigger, stronger and faster than us. On paper they should beat us . . . but boys, we don't play on paper."

The speech was inspiring, but on that fateful day the Brownwood Lions beat the Cisco Lobos on paper, on the field, behind the concession stand, up in the bleachers—you name the surface, they beat us on it.

The principle still holds, however, for implementing a behavior contract with your defiant child; after all the planning, preparing, negotiating and drafting, a contract is still just a piece of paper. And we don't play on paper. Just like a well-practiced football team, a contract comes alive when it's let loose on the field.

To get the ball back from your defiant child and implement a successful behavior contract, you need three vital components: commitment, conviction and consistency.

Commitment

It's been said that the single most significant factor in determining success in any area of life is *commitment*. An individual's strongly held commitment is what turns good intentions into life-changing action.

Commitment is characterized by throwing yourself fully into the task at hand. As someone once said, "With regard to ham and eggs: The chicken is involved, but the pig is committed!" Commitment means not holding anything back, but instead being faithful to do that which you said you would do. God instructs us in the book of Deuteronomy, "And now, O Israel, what does the LORD your God ask of you but to fear the LORD your God, to walk in all his ways, to love him, to serve the LORD your God with all your heart and with all your soul" (10:12). The commitments we make require all our hearts and all our souls.

How were you raised? Were you taught that your word was your bond? That nothing more than a handshake is necessary to seal an agreement? If not, then you missed a wonderful opportunity to learn the art of commitment at a young age. But even if you missed it as a child, a contract is an excellent way to communicate commitment to your defiant teen. By obligating yourself to implement the contract to the letter and then doing so in a loving and faithful manner, you demonstrate that a Christian man or woman of honor always fulfills their commitments.

For a behavior contract to work effectively in your home, you have to commit to implementing it. Decide—long before it's put into practice—that you will be faithful to making this work, that you will be unwavering in your determination to make the contract a success.

It's been said that if you don't stand for something, you'll fall for anything. I believe that old saying is right on the money when it comes to implementing a behavior contract with an extremely defiant child. If you don't stand firm, the defiant teen will make mincemeat out of you and your contract. By contrast, your unshakeable commitment sends the message that things are going to be different around your household. No more business as usual. When your teen sees that you have made this radical commitment to change, it will be a sign that it's okay for them to consider change as well.

Remember this: You set the expectation for change by the level of commitment you show. A steadfast, unwavering commitment to the contract is essential for its success.

Conviction

There are two different types of conviction that are essential to making a contract work.

First, you must execute the contract with great conviction. You might think of this as commitment on steroids. Enforcing the contract with conviction moves it away from mere duty to a level of personal passion. If you're passionate about seeing change in your home, then you should find it easy to be passionate about the contract.

Thomas Edison is a great example of an individual driven by conviction and passion. Perhaps best known as the inventor of the light bulb, he is credited with over 1,000 patents for new inventions during his lifetime.

Edison was a bulldog, unwilling to accept failure as a final outcome to his efforts. Before he successfully invented the alkaline battery, he failed 9,000 times! Edison credited his success to hard work. "Genius is one percent inspiration," Edison said, "and 99 percent perspiration." No one will debate the fact that Edison was a hard worker. He built a laboratory beside his vacation home in Fort Myers, FL, and he is famous for sleeping very little. On his eightieth birthday he announced the formation of a company to do research to develop rubber. He was relentless.[1]

Edison's success has to be credited to more than just determination and willpower. Great people are driven not by pride or strength of will, but by overwhelming conviction and passion.

It is critical that you implement your behavior contract with this same level of conviction and passion. Such an attitude is contagious and can spread like wildfire throughout your home. Passion is alluring, appealing and attractive. We instinctively want to be a part of something passionate. Even if your extremely defiant child shows disdain for anyone who cares enough to be passionate about something, your passion *is* meaningful.

Conviction plays another role in putting the contract into effect: It can be an instrument in the hand of your heavenly Father to convict you of your shortcomings and to encourage you to do your very best to reconcile your child back to Him. This is demonstrated in the book of Acts: "When the people heard this, they were cut to the heart and said to Peter and the other apostles, 'Brothers, what shall we do?'" (2:37). The desire to be used of God in the life of your defiant child should cut you "to the heart" and motivate you to be as useful to Him as possible to bring about healing in your teen's life. Let the contract serve as a constant source of conviction, to remind you of the vital part you can play in bringing reconciliation between your child and the Lord.

Consistency

They say that repetition is the best way to learn, so here I go again: Consistency is absolutely, positively the single greatest factor necessary for the implementation of a successful behavior contract. Bar none, no questions asked, take it to the bank, period. I know I keep saying this, but at least I'm being consistent!

Consistency is about doing what you say you will do, every time, without exception. Consistency and regularity not only lift anxiety for the parent but also give security to the defiant child. Kids need to know what's coming and why it's coming, without much change over time. This sort of consistency is comforting.

Francis Bacon, the famous British statesman and philosopher, understood this concept over 400 years ago when he said, "Look to make your course regular, that men may know beforehand what they may expect." Our kids need to know beforehand what they can expect from us during the discipline process, and consistency gives them that knowledge and security. Your constant, unwavering enforcement of the behavior contract assures them that, under your care, the rules in your home will not be arbitrary and the consequences will not be unpredictable.

Putting the contract into effect is the most critical aspect of the whole process. Moving it off the paper and into real life forces parents to "put up or shut up." I'm convinced that you'll find the behavior contract an invaluable tool to restore calm to your home as carry it out with commitment, conviction and consistency.

To Sum It Up

In this chapter, we discussed the importance of a behavior contract as one of the most powerful tools a parent can use to turn around defiant behavior. It is valuable because it changes the discipline dynamic, helps parents stay on the same page, reduces parental stress, eliminates inconsistency and protects the teen from excessive discipline.

The process of constructing a successful behavior contract includes several steps:

- Setting realistic expectations and reasonable consequences
- Specifying all the areas of expectations, including recent problem behaviors
- Determining your "school zone"
- Simplifying consequences
- Inserting an attitude addendum

- Including the whole family
- Keeping the door open to change
- Starting with all or nothing

We also looked at three keys to making a contract work effectively: commitment, conviction and consistency. Implementing a contract with these components in place ensures that a defiant child gets the message that things are about to change.

HAVE A SEAT ON THE COUCH

1. What do you see as the biggest obstacles to using a behavior contract in your home? How might those be overcome?

2. This chapter listed five reasons that a behavior contract can be valuable in parenting an extremely defiant child. Which of the five reasons most appeals to you? Why?

3. Does putting together a contract seem like a daunting task to you? Why or why not?

4. Did the "helpful hints" ease any anxiety about putting together a contract? Which suggestions do you see as most helpful, or least relevant, to your family?

5. If implementation is the most important aspect of a behavior contract, which of the three components of success do you believe you need the most help with: commitment, conviction or consistency?

8

THE GREAT CONSEQUENCES DEBATE

The most common question parents ask about disciplining their children is, "What are appropriate consequences?" How to successfully motivate a change in behavior is a perplexing question for any parent, but when it comes to determining consequences for an oppositional child—when these choices are being made multiple times a day—the topic can become bewildering. A recurring theme among these beleaguered parents is, "We've tried everything, but nothing seems to work." Whenever the parent dishes out a consequence, the teenager yawns, literally and deliberately, to underscore the message that her parents are impotent when it comes to affecting her behavior.

What Is a Consequence?

I know that starting with a definition can seem a tad elementary, but because this area seems to present a challenge for so many parents, it may help to clearly establish exactly what it is we're talking about.

The dictionary provides three definitions of the noun "consequence":

1. Something that logically flows from an action
2. A logical conclusion
3. The result of a cause[1]

What common thread do we find in all of these definitions? The idea that a consequence results logically from an action. A consequence is directly connected to a choice that was made or an action that was performed.

If a parent's job is to provide consequences for a child's behavior, then we need to understand that the discipline that we lay down *must come as a result* of the child's actions. It needs to be the natural and logical outcome of the choice they made. The opposite of this is true as well: If we do not provide consequences for a child's behavior, then the chain of events tied to that child's action is unnatural and illogical. In the world God created, all of our actions bring consequences. In the life of our children, our job as parents is to be the delivery system of those natural and logical consequences.

What Is the Purpose of Consequences?

Many parents have mistaken ideas about the purpose behind assigning consequences. Paul and Leslie came to me seeking help for dealing with their extremely defiant daughter, Lauren. Now, this girl was something else. Not only had Lauren refused to go to school for months, but she also had blatantly brought alcohol into the home and physically fought anyone who tried to take it from her. She disappeared for hours at a time, often coming home in the wee hours before dawn, and never deemed it necessary to communicate anything but disgust and disdain for her parents.

Leslie was appalled by her daughter's actions and even more appalled by her husband's weak, ineffective response. After Paul had recounted for me another harrowing episode from the previous night, I asked this well-meaning father what consequences his daughter would receive as a result of her grossly inappropriate actions. He told me, "I believe my talking with her about what she did is consequence enough."

When I asked Paul to define for me what he saw as the purpose of consequences, he explained that he viewed them as a means to help curb the negative behavior of the child. My guess is that you're already anticipating my next question. Respectfully, I asked, "So, Paul, how has your choice of consequences been working for you? Do you see your daughter curbing her behavior as a result of you just talking with her about her inappropriate actions?"

He looked at me sort of like a preschooler looks at a quadratic equation . . . without comprehension. I don't think that he'd ever considered the question before.

The purpose of consequences is *to motivate a defiant teen to make good choices in life*. If consequences are the natural and logical result of a person's behavior, then the concept goes both ways. Our children should know that the logical result of good behavior on their part is an outpouring of goodwill, blessings untold and a nearly unlimited menu of activities they can enjoy as a member of the family. But they also need to know *and experience* that the logical result of bad behavior is that free-flow of blessings practically dries up.

This is, of course, a purely biblical concept. The notion that all our actions bring a natural result is present in New Testament teaching, and it reverberates all the way back to Job, the most ancient book in the entire Bible. Here is just a sampling of what God wants us to know about consequences:

> As I have observed, those who plow evil and those who sow trouble reap it (Job 4:8).

> He who sows wickedness reaps trouble, and the rod of his fury will be destroyed (Prov. 22:8).

> The wicked man earns deceptive wages, but he who sows righteousness reaps a sure reward (Prov. 11:18).

> Tell the righteous it will be well with them, for they will enjoy the fruit of their deeds (Isa. 3:10).

> Do not be deceived: God cannot be mocked. A man reaps what he sows (Gal. 6:7).

If you take a little time to read through your Bible, you'll quickly see that the steadfast principle of consequences has been a central theme of God's interaction with humans from the very beginning. When Adam and Eve defied the one rule God set for living in the Garden, the natural result was their fall from grace and their loss of daily, intimate fellowship with Him. And because of God's holy character, humanity's sins required the ultimate consequence of His own Son being butchered on the cross. So you might say that God takes the idea of consequences rather seriously. And, as we've discussed before, we need to take seriously everything that God takes seriously. Because God makes sure that we experience consequences to help us see the value in following Jesus, it is mandatory that we make sure our kids experience consequences for the exact same reason.

A Cost-Benefit Analysis

Throughout this chapter, I'll be using the analogy of speeding tickets to illustrate the concept of consequences. Now, just because I own a convertible, live out in the country and have a long, winding commute into the office each day, doesn't mean that I receive a lot of speeding tickets. (Of course, I suppose that depends on how you define "a lot.")

For our discussion, let's propose this hypothetical situation: What if all speeding tickets came with a $1.00 fine? Let's say that no matter how far you exceeded the speed limit, all tickets would cost just $1.00 apiece. How fast would you drive? Would you always obey the posted speed limit? Think of how fast you could run your errands and get to and from work! Would paying a $1.00 fine be worth all that time saved? Okay, let's have a show of hands. How many would always drive the speed limit? Uh-huh, yes . . . I see that hand. God bless you, any others?

Now, how many of you would most likely exceed the speed limit because the fine for doing so was so small? Wow! Since you're all sitting in that recliner in your home alone reading this book, I can see we have many honest people out there.

In the exercise above, you conducted a cost-benefit analysis of the situation. In response to my question, you asked yourself, "Does the benefit of driving faster outweigh the cost of the fine? Or, does the cost of the fine outweigh the benefit of driving faster?" For many people, the answer would be A. Oh, who are we kidding? In the scenario we described, the number of speeders would be more like "everyone." If speeding tickets were $1.00, the highways in this country would look like the German Autobahn! We might as well paint big numbers on our car hoods and send our kids to Daytona for drivers ed!

So what is it that currently keeps our highways from looking like the Indy 500? That's right: the simple fact that speeding tickets are not anywhere close to $1.00. Believe it or not, your defiant teen, math whiz or no, conducts a cost-benefit analysis on a regular basis. He tries to determine whether the action he is about to take is worth the corresponding consequences.

Earlier in the book, I promised to revisit a couple of stories, so let's do that now. Both of these examples demonstrate that teenagers are surprisingly skilled at cost-benefit analyses. First, do you remember how I won the contest at my junior-high school by getting 64 licks in the eighth grade? Most of those came at the hands of my English teacher, Mrs. Hart (no pun intended . . . okay, maybe a slight pun intended). Mrs. Hart was a very nice woman, and my behavior in her class had nothing to do with her abilities as a teacher or her qualities as a wonderful person. It's just that her method of motivation wasn't very . . . effective. Whenever she took me out in the hall to paddle me, she'd say, "Jimmy, I'm sorry to have to do this. You know this hurts me more than it hurts you." And on these occasions, I actually believe she was telling the truth. When she brought the paddle down, it felt like a monarch butterfly had landed on my rear end. Bless her heart, she really was trying to mold me into a nice young man, but her discipline lacked the one ingredient it would have taken to get the job done: upper body strength. The punishment brought no pain, so the punishment didn't deter future poor behavior.

The second story I promised to return to centered on Eric, the client who refused to speak in session. As you may remember, this teenager was very polite—he simply refused to speak to me because he had promised his parents that he wouldn't speak if they brought him in. Eric's parents responded with several big-time consequences, such as grounding him from associating with friends and revoking all of his electronics privileges until he came to counseling and spoke to me during his session.

The next time they brought him back, Eric spoke. He said, "I'm speaking to you now, am I not? So you can tell my parents that I spoke to you more than I did the last time, right?" Then he clammed up for the next 40-give minutes. You have to hand it to him: He was certainly giving it the old college try. But his parents had turned over a new leaf. The behavior contract they'd created specified that he must fully engage in the counseling process in order to win back his privileges. Because Eric violated the terms, he remained cut off from friends and any electronic entertainment for another week.

During his third visit to my office, Eric showed himself to be a remarkably talkative young man. In his personal cost-benefit analysis of the situation, he determined that the cost of his negative behavior didn't outweigh the benefits until the third week of consequences. When he decided that his actions were costing more than he was willing to pay, he conformed his behavior.

So what do we learn from speeding tickets, the less-than-hearty discipline of Mrs. Hart, and the transformation of young Eric? We learn that *consequences have to hurt to help*. This takes us back to our earlier discussion about the necessity of giving defiant teens a reason to choose a different behavior. We have to provide an external motivator of sufficient magnitude to stimulate them to make better choices. If a consequence does not rise to the level of inflicting significant pain, the child will see no reason to change his behavior.

I was leading a parenting conference in Dallas when the discussion turned to various ideas for successful consequences. About halfway through the dialogue I remember saying, "Wow, if someone walked in right now, all they would hear us talking about is how to cause our children pain!" But truly, as harsh as it sounds, the fact remains that consequences have to hurt to help. As we learn from Mrs. Hart's paddlings and Paul's futile talks with his daughter about what she did wrong, consequences that don't bring some form of pain will not be effective in reducing the negative behavior of a defiant teen. And reducing negative behavior is the entire purpose of setting consequences in the first place.

What Makes a Consequence Effective?

So what will get your child's attention? What consequence carries enough persuasive power to entice your child to reconsider his or her defiant behavior? That's a question only you can answer, because only you know your child. This may sound like a cop-out on my part, but it is nonetheless true.

Fifteen-year-old Lonnie provides an excellent example. An avid gamer, he has several gaming systems and spends hours a day honing his skills as a Rogue with stealth abilities and great damage-inflicting potential. (If you know what that means, you're way ahead of me.) During the intake portion of our first session, I asked Lonnie who his best friend was. He named Robert. "Is Robert a school friend or a church friend?" I asked. Lonnie replied that he was neither, so I enquired further. "Does he live in your neighborhood?"

"No, he lives in New York City," Lonnie said. "He's in my clan on my online fantasy role-playing game and we spend hours together every day. He's awesome!" Not only did Lonnie consider a boy (if he truly was a boy. Chances are Robert was a 55-year-old truck driver from Pensacola) he'd never met before to be his best friend, he didn't have very many friends in real life. He was sort of a social recluse.

If you were Lonnie's parent, what would you do if he violated an agreed-upon boundary? Ground him? That's certainly one option, but it seems like his life would continue pretty much unimpeded if that happened. Take away his cell phone? Sure, but he only uses it to call his parents or Game Stop. Again, no real pain in losing that privilege. Chances are, taking away his electronics would be the quickest way to get Lonnie's attention, because that's what he cares about the most. Taking away his "fantasy world" for several days would definitely hurt, so it would probably help.

But what about the 16-year-old social butterfly who spends every moment possible away from home, hanging out with friends and attending social gatherings at school or church? We're talking about the girl whose parents have to pry the cell phone out of her hand or she'll stay on it until the sun comes up? How would taking away video games affect her? Probably not much, if at all. But if she were grounded from seeing her friends or if her cell phone was confiscated for a period of time, life would come to an abrupt halt and she'd definitely take notice.

Every child is different. Only you know what will carry a sufficiently negative impact to cause your child to reconsider his or her defiant behavior, so only you can determine what makes for an effective
consequence.

One mother came into my office completely discouraged because
nothing seemed to work with her 12-year-old son. Ellen said that she
had taken away everything she could think of, but her son just laid on
his bed, seemingly impervious to her attempts at discipline. She said
that there was nothing else to try, because her son didn't care about
anything. Now, that may be true for some kids. I have met some teenage
clients who come close to not caring about anything; their hearts are so
hardened and their consciences so calloused that they've lost social perspective and are perhaps anti-social or even sociopathic. But such kids
are an extremely small minority of defiant teens, and Ellen's son was
definitely not one of them. I implored her to watch her son. What does
he do, where does he go, what does he spend his time doing?

She returned to my office the next week elated. "I found it!" she declared. "I finally found a consequence that will get his attention: Take
away his hair gel!" In observing her child more closely, she had noticed
that he spent a good 20 minutes in front of the mirror each morning,
getting his hairdo just right. Apparently, when his mother took away
his hair gel as a consequence for violating an agreed-upon boundary,
you'd have thought she sentenced him to the electric chair. I was surprised to hear her describe such a big impact from such a seemingly
small consequence—until the boy walked into my office.

Do you remember back in high school science class when we
learned about static electricity? The teacher would get this big silver
ball and select a student to hold the ball with both hands. Pretty soon,
every hair on the student's head would be standing on end. Well, that
was pretty much what this youngster looked like when he sheepishly
entered the room. Clearly, that hair gel played an important role in his
young life. The mother reported that his behavior improved dramatically after she implemented this innovative new discipline strategy.

No one knows your child like you do. What does he care about the
most? What receives her most passionate interest? When you figure out

what will upset your teen the most, then you have probably found the most effective consequence.

Now the question is, how can you most effectively put that consequence into action?

Make It Short but Severe

I'm a pretty big believer in employing stern discipline choices but limiting their duration to a fairly short term. For example, let's say that the "school zone" you've identified for your defiant teen is acting disrespectfully to authority figures. Violating that boundary earns your teen Lock Down. Lock Down, in this particular case, might mean no electronics and no interaction with anyone outside the family. "No electronics" means no TV, no mp3 players, no computers, no video game systems, no stereos, no cell phones, no house phones, no portable DVD players, no CD players. If it has batteries, a screen or plugs in, your child will not be using it.

You might think that's a pretty harsh consequence, since the child will be left with nothing but an Etch-A-Sketch and a three-month-old copy of *Tiger Beat* magazine to while away the hours. However, this harsh sentence will be served for a relatively short time. You can decide that Lock Down will last for only, let's say, 48 hours, and then she gets back all of her goodies. The goal is for her to think, when it's all over, something like this: *That was horrible! That was the most painful ordeal I've ever experienced. I couldn't talk with my friends. I couldn't keep up with the latest reality show featuring several inane, wealthy teenagers and their narcissistic mothers in Southern California. It was horrifying!*

The downside was enduring a rather severe consequence, but the upside was receiving parole in just two days. Will she remember how bad it felt? Will she be able to recall her sense of isolation from friends the next time she is tempted to act disrespectfully to her parents? It would be reasonable to anticipate that as a strong possibility. But if not, that 48-hour Lock Down can easily be increased to three days or five days, depending on the teenager's future choices. In general, short but severe consequences tend to be fairly effective.

Alternative Consequences

When most parents think *consequences,* they think of taking something away. When teenagers act up, their parents often turn to the old reliable penalties: grounding them from various activities, taking their phone away or restricting their TV watching. Most parental choices in America, a culture adrift in a sea of material gluttony, involve some form of deprivation. Why? Because most parents find that removing some favored possession or activity is an attention-getter that tends to sufficiently motivate their kids to make more appropriate choices.

But if taking away privileges or possessions is the only club in your bag, then you're playing at a disadvantage. Your consequence choices are somewhat limited. So let's consider some alternative consequences that parents I've worked with have found to be quite effective.

One suggestion is to try giving your child something rather than taking something away. For example, if your 15-year-old has difficulty telling the truth, assign him a 10-page research paper on lying. What is it? What various forms of lying do people engage in? What are the long- and short-term ramifications of not telling the truth? This paper should be double-spaced, set in Times New Roman 12-point type, and include no less than 10 cited sources. (Obviously, this might not be a good fit for younger kids, but you get the idea.)

Another option is to give the child a task he finds especially distasteful. This might be cleaning out garage, weeding the backyard or maybe scrubbing the toilets.

Your child will not likely jump for joy at these unexpected "gifts," so as motivation to complete the task, you can place the child on total Lock Down until the job is completed. The length of the consequence is completely up to him. If you still prefer to take things away, however, I'd like to suggest some discipline choices that many parents never consider. Here are some "takeaways" that my clients have shared with me:

- Delete songs off your teen's mp3 library.
- Remove some favorite clothing items from the wardrobe, leaving nothing but generic bargain brands or outdated styles your child wouldn't want to be caught dead in.

- Cut off access to MySpace or Facebook for a certain set number of days.
- Remove texting capabilities from the teen's cell phone for a length of time.

This is certainly not an exhaustive list of creative discipline possibilities, but I hope these examples will get your creative juices flowing.

Common Consequence Mistakes

One of the reasons parents are so often frustrated when trying to determine good and effective consequences is that they make mistakes in how they implement the discipline. No matter how great a consequence choice may be, if it is not executed correctly, then its effectiveness can be all but nullified.

Don't fall prey to the most common consequence mistakes parents make.

Alter the Consequences

Rhonda had finally put her foot down and told her daughter that she was grounded for the next three days. Their contract stipulated that this was the penalty for lying to a parent, so that was the consequence Abby would receive. When she broke this news to her daughter, the 16-year-old pitched a walleyed fit. She went on and on about how unfair this was and declared that she would never forgive her mother for ruining her life.

Abby's despair was provoked not so much by the grounding itself, but by the fact that her consequence would last over Saturday night. This particular Saturday night just happened to be reserved for the biggest party of the year. Abby couldn't believe that she'd even been invited, and now her mother was destroying what little hope she had of being slightly popular at school.

She pleaded her case with Rhonda: "Mom, you know how important this party is for me. You even said that it was a great honor and how proud you were that so many kids liked me. Well, if I don't show at this party, I'm ruined; they'll think that I'm rude and stuck up. Come on, Mom, please? You can ground me for three additional days next week, but you just have to let me go to this party. It's a matter of life and death!"

After a long pause and some considerable thought, Rhonda said, "Okay, young lady, but you're not going anywhere next Monday through Wednesday, understand?"

This mom had such a great opportunity to let her daughter experience the painful consequences of making a bad choice. She had the chance to communicate to her child the importance of being honest, being honorable and always telling the truth. Instead, she gave her daughter a wet noodle response that caused very little pain at all. I mean, what was Abby's agenda for Monday through Wednesday night anyway? That's right, staying at home.

Remember: The first rule of consequences is that they have to hurt to help. We *want* this child to miss an event during the grounding. That's the point. This is all about the child and the choices she made. Abby knew the consequences for lying to her mother *and* she knew the party fell within those three days—yet she chose to lie anyway. When she chose not to tell the truth, she chose to miss the party.

It's imperative that parents do not back off the consequences once they've been assigned. The more a negative behavior costs the child, the more likely her cost-benefit analysis will lead to a different decision next time. If Abby had missed that party, she'd likely be much more motivated to tell the truth in the future.

If Consequences Don't Seem to Be Working, Just Give Up

Cynthia has repeatedly grounded her son for acting disrespectfully, but he just keeps on doing it. Out of frustration, she exclaims, "Nothing works with that kid. It doesn't matter what consequences we give him, nothing motivates him to make better choices. I'd just as soon not have all the arguing and fighting that comes when I try to discipline him. I guess I'll just leave him alone, if he'll leave me alone."

Any parent of an extremely defiant child can understand this mother's frustration and feelings of hopelessness. Exhausted and discouraged, she's losing hope that things will ever change. But yielding to defiance is never the solution to defiance.

Let's go back to the traffic ticket scenario for a moment. Let's say that I get one speeding ticket a week for an entire month. The same highway patrolman keeps giving me tickets, and he's getting frustrated that I don't seem to be getting the message to slow down. At the end of the month, he and the other patrolmen are discussing the situation. He finally says, "Well, even though he keeps getting tickets, he doesn't seem to be slowing down. I guess giving him tickets is just not going to motivate him to make better driving choices, so let's just stop giving him any. Let's just let him drive as fast as he can, as often as he likes, because I'm tired of the hassle."

If law enforcement took this attitude with lawbreakers, society couldn't function. We'd have pandemonium on the streets. We don't reward constant rule violators by ending all consequences for their actions. What kind of a message would that send? Resist long enough and you'll get off scot-free!

Certainly, the purpose of consequences is to curb negative behavior, but a greater purpose is at work as well. Parents need to make sure that their children receive negative consequences for negative behavior simply because *it is the right thing to do*. Whether it works or not, whether it seems to be getting their attention or not, we make sure that they experience painful compensation for defiant choices because we are instilling a vital life principle: No matter who you are, no matter what you believe and no matter how long it takes for you to learn this lesson, you *will* reap what you sow. Actions have consequences.

Even if you don't see immediate results from all your hard parenting choices, don't give up hope. No matter how your defiant child responds to the consequences, you are fulfilling your charge before God by providing them.

Rely Solely on Negative Discipline

When Peter came into my office, he was so angry at his parents that he couldn't stand it. "They grounded me again! Can you believe it? And it's for something totally stupid." Apparently, he'd been talking to his buddy Mike after his phone curfew. Peter's parents want him off his cell phone by 10 PM. "Ten o'clock! Nobody has to get off their phones by 10. Why are they treating me like Charles Manson just because I didn't get off the phone on time?"

Peter's rant continued as he pointed out that he'd made all *B*s on his report card, but his parents didn't even seem to notice. He did his chores around the house without being asked, which is more than he can say for his younger brother and sister, but his parents hadn't even given him one measly "way to go."

"All they focus on are the negatives! When are they going to give me some credit for the good things that I do?"

As a parent struggling to raise an extremely defiant child, you may find positive responses hard to come by. Most of your energy is spent fighting the good fight to rein in your child's constant attempts to violate rules and usurp your authority. But as we mentioned earlier in the book, the pattern of negative communication that often develops between parents and a defiant teen can wear away at the fabric of the parent-child relationship to the point that it becomes tattered almost beyond repair.

Always remember that discipline—guiding your child toward better choices—is a two-way street. Yes, it encompasses giving negative consequences for unacceptable behavior, but it also includes encouraging and praising your defiant child for doing something right. Seize every opportunity to heap praise on your teenager for achieving any level of success. Offer encouragement through words of warmth and support every chance you get, remembering that those chances may be few and far between. Your child desperately needs to know that you still believe in him, that you still see good in him and that you still expect success from him. Try not to get caught up in constant negativism. Instead, aim to discipline just as much—if not more—with praise than with punishment.

By the way, I do not believe that support and encouragement come from paying children for being helpful around the house—this happens to be a pet peeve of mine. As we discussed earlier, parents today are fighting a constant battle to reduce their children's sense of entitlement and selfishness and promote a spirit of gratitude and appreciation. If the only way you can persuade a teenager to clean up that cluttered bedroom or mow the lawn is to offer a $20 bribe, then you are defeating your own efforts.

I believe it sets a bad precedent to reward or pay a child for what should be considered normal, cooperative behavior. No policeman has ever stopped me on the street, given me a $100-bill and thanked me for not robbing a bank today. The choice to *not* rob a bank is an expected, normal behavior for a member of our society, and I don't get rewarded for it. In the same way, helping around the house, washing the car or mowing the lawn is the sort of cooperation normally expected of any member of the household. Moms work around the house, so do dads and so should every member of the family. And last time I checked, Mom didn't get 20 bucks for vacuuming the dining room!

Besides, your teen already gets paid for helping around the house. It's called central heat and air, food, clothing, toiletries and all the water they can drink. Now, if you want to pay her something extra for helping to paint the garage or another out-of-the-ordinary job, that's fine. But normal house chores come with the territory of living in a family. Kids help out around the house because it's the right thing to do.

What your defiant teen needs to earn by joining in with the family to accomplish family responsibilities is praise, encouragement and sense that they are a source of joy to you.

Extend Grace Way Too Often

Here are just a few examples of the reasoning parents give for minimizing a child's consequences:

- "I know you're supposed to be grounded for a week, but you've been so good, let's just make it three days."

- "Listen, I know your father said that you couldn't have your phone for three days, but go ahead . . . here. I want to hear what happened between Joey and Christi, so give her a call. Oh, and don't tell your dad."

- "You know the contract says that you're supposed to be in tutoring after school if you fail a class, but the team called a special practice. Since I'm the coach, I've decided that I need you there. But just this once, you hear me?"

Back to speeding tickets for a second. Beth, my wife, never gets them. I could probably count on one hand the amount of traffic tickets she has received in all the years we've been married. Now, don't get the wrong idea. It's not that she's a good driver. Far from it. In fact, she's been pulled over for speeding about as many times as I have, and she even ran a stop sign once—in front of the police station!

But what happens when she gets pulled over? She bats her baby blue eyes at the police officer, claims ignorance and gets handed a warning almost every time. On those rare occasions when Beth does receive a citation, she gets upset that that police would have the audacity to actually give her a ticket. She is so used to being let off the hook that when someone actually keeps her on the hook, she feels wronged.

And what about me? In all the years we've been married, I can count on one or two fingers the number of warnings I've received, but I'd have to take off my shoes to add up my citations. I must look like a Colombian drug lord or something, because they have the ticket half written by the time they get to my window. On those rare and glorious occasions when that nice, saint-like policeman gives me a warning, I am overcome with gratitude. It's like the heavens have opened up and manna is falling down. What an unexpected gift! I truly understand the meaning of grace.

Now, what does this foray into self-incrimination (and spouse-incrimination) have to do with our discussion? It reveals what can happen when parents dish out grace on a regular basis.

Extending Grace Too Often Can Trigger Anger in the Defiant Child
A child who is used to receiving grace all the time is lulled into believing that consequences will never come. She thinks, *If mom lets an offense slide once, why wouldn't she let it slide every time?* And when you *do* try to enforce the consequences, she feels enraged that you would be

so unfair as to make her pay the agreed-upon price when you didn't do so last time. When your child comes to expect grace as the rule instead of the exception, you are creating more opportunity for future anger episodes.

Extending grace too often can trigger anger for another reason as well. It can make the defiant child feel that you don't consider him worth the effort to enforce the rules. A 17-year-old sat in my office crying and wondering aloud, "Why don't my parents grow some &^%$ [show some guts] and make me do what I'm supposed to do?!" He interpreted his parents' over-use of grace as a sign that he was not worth the trouble it took to enforce the rules. Countless kids have told me that they wished their parents cared enough to ask them to call or to check up on them or to be angry when they break a rule. They say, "Everyone thinks I have the cool parents. My parents aren't cool . . . they just don't care." As ironic as it may sound, when used too often, grace can provoke anger in your defiant child.

Extending Grace Too Often Can Nullify Its Meaning

We have talked about cheap grace before, but it bears repeating. When you show your child grace too often, it becomes the rule, not the exception. For some reason, parents tend to believe that a child who receives grace in a particular situation will understand that grace was given, will appreciate the gesture and will reciprocate in kind. Because you did something nice for her, she'll now be nice to you. But kids who experience grace too often don't appreciate it for the gift it is. A defiant teen doesn't look at her parents with appreciation for their kindness; she looks at them with contempt for their weakness. When asked who wins the power struggle in their house, virtually every defiant teen I have ever worked with says, "I always win." In order for grace to be effective and to communicate the message you intend, it must be the rare exception to the rule. Grace is most effective when a child has paid the price for her actions 99 consecutive times, and on the one-hundredth occasion, she is shown grace. Under those circumstances, she will be much more likely to understand the concept and appreciate what you are doing for her.

The Nuclear Option

I deliberately saved this section for last because the consequence we're about to discuss should be used only as a final choice after a parent has tried all other options to no avail. The "nuclear option" is a consequence reserved only for those kids who have continued to defy the authority of their parents, with no signs of ever changing their behavior. We're talking here about removing the teen from the home for a prolonged period of time.

For some families, there may come a time when, because of continual defiant, criminal or violent behavior, a child must be removed, sometimes forcibly, from the home. You may be thinking that such a consequence crosses the line of acceptable parental choices. It may violate your moral sense as a loving Christian parent, and you're convinced that no reasonable person would even consider entertaining such a thought.

Let's look once again at Lauren, one of the most defiant teens I have ever worked with. As you remember, this 16-year-old completely ignored her parents, refused to attend school and came and went from the house with complete impunity. On the rare occasions her parents, Paul and Leslie, tried to curb her behavior, Lauren became physically violent. She would slap and scratch her parents until they got out of the way. Then she left the house and did as she pleased, and came home when she pleased. Most of the time, she drove home just before dawn, either drunk or high on weed.

During one family session with Lauren and her parents, I suggested that, given her violent, criminal behavior, removal from the home might be the only option her parents had left for trying to motivate a change in her behavior. Lauren's father interrupted me to state, in no uncertain terms, that he would *never*, under *any* circumstances, kick his daughter out of his home. He declared that he would never be party to such an unloving, unchristian act.

Less than a month later, father and daughter were in my office following yet another violent and unbelievably rebellious weekend encounter. Paul summoned the gumption to tell her, "I have had it, young lady. I will not allow you to treat me or your mother that way again."

This 16-year-old child stared her father down and asked in a cold, menacing tone, "And just what are you going to do about it?"

You know something? That was a great question. What *was* the dad going to do about it? When you take removal from the home off the table, then you are ultimately restricted in your options with dealing with an exceptionally defiant child. A child needs to know that, if all other attempts fail, the privilege of living with the family can be removed as well.

Just today, a mom called to tell me she was ready to take drastic measures. The fall school semester has just started here in Austin, and for the third straight semester, her daughter has refused to attend school. She has refused to attend school, refused to do any work sent home by the school and refused to complete any Internet-assisted homeschool curriculum. Her parents had believed that she would eventually move through this phase on her own—that she would come to her senses or just get tired of staying at home watching TV. But they are now approaching the one-year mark of dealing with their daughter's refusal to comply with their directions, and those of school officials and law enforcement.

This is another example of how insanity is doing the same thing over and over again but expecting different results. When I met with her, I noticed that the girl herself seemed surprised that her parents allowed her to stay home for as long as she has. If these parents chose to continue down the path they've followed for the past year, then a year from now, their daughter might still be holed up in the family room.

Although she has long opposed the idea of having her child placed in residential treatment, the mom told me today that the time had come: "She has refused to comply for the last time. We have no choice but to place her where she can get some help." In the life of some of the most defiant of teens, removal from the home is an absolutely necessary option for parents.

A Three-Tiered Approach to Removal

I suggest a three-tiered approach to consequences with an extremely defiant teenager. Each of these levels should be clearly explained and delineated in the contract so that there can be no misunderstanding or ambiguity.

- **Tier 1: Implementation of the contract.** Installing the contract is your first decisive step in giving your defiant child firm yet reasonable boundaries. If the child refuses to comply with the contract and constantly breaks the rules, it's time to implement Tier 2.

- **Tier 2: Increased consequences for contract violations.** The contract needs to state that after repeated violations, the consequences outlined in the contract will be increased. For example, if the contract originally called for three days of grounding if the teen missed a curfew, that consequence will be increased to five days if that rule is violated twice during the same month. If you have increased consequences once, or maybe twice, with no change in behavior, then Tier 3 kicks in.

- **Tier 3: Removal from the home.** This is strike three. The teen has received at least two other stern warnings. Other, less drastic consequences have been ignored, so the child has made the choice to be removed from the home.

Removal from the home has to be the end of a long line of attempts on the part of the parents to motivate the child to make better, more positive behavioral choices. But it has to be included, or the extremely defiant child has the parent over a barrel.

A Fine Line, But an Important One

If you ever face this terrible decision, I believe that it is vital to make clear that this action is being taken because of your child's choices, not because of the frustration, anger or exasperation you feel as parents. I always tell parents to clearly communicate this to their teen. The conversation could go something like this:

I will never, ever kick you out of this house. This is your home, and I would never do that. But you can choose not to live here. And by continuing to defy our authority and continuing to break the agreed-upon contract, you are choosing not to live here. This has nothing to do with us and everything to do with you and your choices. Remember when we said that choices bring about consequences? We've warned you for some time that this could ultimately be the consequence of your continued rebelliousness, and for some reason you have chosen to leave our home. This saddens us to no end, but it was your choice. You are now going to suffer the consequences we said would come. We're so sorry that you've made this choice, but we know that God has His plan, and you're going to a place where they can give you more help than we apparently can provide.

To Where Will the Teen Be Removed?

Removal from the home cannot mean moving the teen to a situation he or she desires. As we've seen, consequences need to bring pain if they're going to bring change. What will motivate a child to change if his extremely defiant behavior results in his going to live with one of his friends with sympathetic parents or moving in with a relative who sets fewer restrictions? These moves actually pay off for the child and completely undermine the whole purpose of removal.

An extremely defiant child whose choices have led to removal from the home must be placed in a very negative circumstance that demonstrates the gravity of this most severe consequence.

There are two basic types of facilities where an incorrigible teen may be placed: a therapeutic facility or a highly structured boarding facility. Let's take a quick look at each.

A therapeutic facility is just what the name suggests: a place where the child will receive medical, counseling or other therapeutic intervention. The purpose of these places is to get to the bottom of the aberrant behavior and work toward a positive change. This type of program also comes in several forms.

- **A medical model.** If your child's aberrant behavior is related to a medical or neurological issue, then all the consequences in the world will not be effective. A medical model facility diagnoses and treats these medical conditions to help restore the child to good mental health. These facilities tend to be used after all other courses of actions have been tried, such as intensive outpatient programs. This type of program tends to be the most expensive.

- **A behavioral model.** These programs may include medical supervision, but for the most part, the staff's expertise is dealing with kids whose issues are not primarily medical but behavioral in nature. Many wilderness camps fall into this category. This type of program tends to be slightly less expensive.

A structured boarding facility does not provided much in the way of therapy or counseling for the child. They exist to provide a highly structured living and learning environment for a child or teen away from home. These programs generally include academic studies and athletics, and may also include group and family counseling in some cases. Such boarding programs still cost money, but they are by and large the cheaper option.

What About the Cost?

This is the $64,000 question. And in some cases, it is quite literally $64,000. If you were to pay cash for most of these programs, the price would be way out of reach for all but the wealthiest parents. The good news is that many insurance companies will pay most, if not all, of the cost of some programs. In addition, Medicaid pays for some, and many facilities receive funding from government or private sources, so they can charge what a family is able to pay. Your state has many options available, so don't think money puts a residential program out of reach for you and your family.

The decision to remove an extremely defiant child from the home is drastic, but this option is, many times, a vitally important one. As painful as the decision may be, we must remember that it is the logical result of the child's behavioral choices, and that it may be the first step toward getting him or her the more intensive help he or she desperately needs.

Having the child separated from his family may seem unloving, but in the most extreme cases, it is actually the most loving act a parent can take for their extremely defiant teen. Life will teach him, in some harsh and brutal ways, that negative consequences come with negative behavior. It should be every parent's goal to do whatever it takes to ingrain this principle into his or her child's psyche before that child leaves home. Whatever it takes.

To Sum It Up

In this chapter, we learned that a consequence is something that logically or naturally flows from a particular choice or action. Just as God gives us consequences to remind us of the value of following Jesus, parents should ensure that consequences motivate their teens to make positive behavioral choices.

Since consequences have to hurt to help, choosing an effective consequence for a defiant teen involves knowing what will have the biggest impact, given the child's interest and priorities. Well-chosen consequences may be severe in nature, but they can be quite effective even with a short-term sentence. Trying alternative, creative consequences may help get the child's attention.

Even effective consequences can be undermined by common parenting mistakes. Don't:

- Alter the consequence
- Just give up if the consequence doesn't seem to be working
- Rely solely on negative discipline
- Extend grace way too often

Finally, we spoke about removing the extremely defiant teen from the home as the final option in the arsenal of every parent of a defiant teen. As difficult as this choice may be, it may be exactly the motivation some children need to help change their behavior.

A Quick Follow-up

Back to Lauren and her parents, Paul and Leslie. As you may have already guessed, things did not turn out well for this family. Dad continued to make excuses for his daughter's behavior and continued to belittle his wife for wanting to take appropriate disciplinary steps. He worked against every measure that was put into place, and continued to paint his wife as the reason for all the anger and conflict in his home. The last time I saw, them Leslie was asking for a legal separation from Paul and the conflict in their home was progressing unabated. At the time of this writing, Lauren would be about 19 now. Last time I heard, her parents had no idea where she was.

HAVE A SEAT ON THE COUCH

1. What do you find to be the most difficult aspect of determining and implementing effective consequences for your child? Why?

2. Since you know your child best, what consequences do you believe work best for him or her? What consequences would be least effective? Why?

3. How did you react to the idea that a consequence has to hurt to help? Does that seem mean to you, or does it sound practical? Explain your response.

4. Which of the four most common mistakes that parents make with consequences hit closest to home with you? Why?

5. How did you feel as you read the section on removing a defiant teen from the home? Does even considering this as a possible last-choice option make you feel uncomfortable? Why? Why not?

9

DON'T LET YOUR MARRIAGE BECOME COLLATERAL DAMAGE

Bill and Lilly were in my office for the very first time. They had come in seeking help for their 14-year-old son, David, who had explosive anger episodes and was failing at school. They feared he also was experimenting with drug use. But less than five minutes into our session, I realized that David's defiance was not the primary issue in this family. Take a look at some excerpts from our conversation and see if you can identify the real problem:

- "Bill is never home and pretty much just leaves me to raise the kids alone."

- "She rides the kids all the time. She never lets up. I think she's responsible for most of his blow-ups."

- "I'm tired of always being the bad guy. *He* just wants to be David's buddy all the time. Well, news flash: You're his father, not his buddy! It's like I have to parent Bill as if he's my child as well!"

- "Lilly is just crushing our son! If we lose him, she will be the reason."

The biggest challenge confronting this couple was not their defiant son, but their own dysfunctional relationship. As with so many of the couples who come into my office, the marriage was in just as much trouble as the child, if not more.

So is this just a coincidence, or is there a direct connection between defiant teens and parents with poor marriage relationships? Based on my experience, the two are definitely connected; however, identifying one as the cause of the other is more of a stretch. The situation resembles the age old question of which came first—the chicken or the egg? Does a bad marriage contribute to the development of a defiant child, or is a defiant child the catalyst that produces dysfunction within a marriage relationship? The answer is, of course, is a little bit of both.

In my practice, I have seen many couples whose marriages are in such poor shape that bitterness and dysfunction flow from the two of them like poison spreading to the other members of the family. But I've seen an equal number of fairly solid marriage relationships that, when forced to run the gauntlet of parenting an extremely defiant teen, succumb to bitterness and dysfunction. In this chapter, we're not going to focus on the origins of this predicament; instead, we're going to examine the typical effects and look at some ways to protect your marriage from becoming collateral damage in your battle with a defiant teen.

My Particular Interest

As I've said, I frequently witness the fallout from damaged marriages that are in some way connected to the presence of a defiant teen in the home. My heart always goes out to these couples, because I understand how difficult it can be to raise an extremely defiant child, much less how it must feel as if you are suffering through this trauma alone because your marriage is struggling. I was so struck by this issue that when it was time to pick a dissertation topic for my doctoral work, I chose, without hesitation, to examine how parenting a defiant child impacts the marriage relationship. In reviewing the available literature, I was surprised by how little research had been done on the subject. Tons of articles examined how poor parenting impacts the behavior of children, but very little, if any, research had been conducted on how a child's behavior can impact the parents' marriage.

I wanted to get a snapshot of how raising an exceptionally defiant child affects a healthy marriage relationship. So I designed my research study to involve only couples with no history of previous marital difficulties who at the time were parenting teenagers diagnosed with and being treated for Oppositional Defiant Disorder, with no other co-morbid disorders such as bipolar disorder or depression.

In this chapter, I'll be sharing with you some of the results of that research study, which gave me some unique insights into the hearts and minds of married couples trying desperately to raise an extremely defiant teenager.

Common Characteristics of Husbands in Homes of Defiant Teens

One of the more remarkable aspects of the study was how many parents of defiant teens exhibited the same kinds of behaviors, almost across the board. Let's look first at some characteristics shared by the majority of the husbands in these homes.

Passive and Conflict Avoidant

Let me quote directly from the study results:

> The most striking and prevalent revelation that emerged from the interviews and the perception of the researcher was the number of husbands who were weak-willed, ineffectual, unengaged, conflict avoidant, or passive in their interactions with their wives and children. This attitude was more common than any other and was a commonality among all but one of the participants.[1]

This characteristic was true of all but one of the participating husbands! One wife in the study summarized her husband's behavior like this: "There are conflicts where he will not go there. He just won't go there." It blew me away to learn that this was the single most common characteristic shared by families with extremely defiant teens. The results of the study, however, were unmistakable.

But why? Why would a father's passivity be such a consistent factor in the marriage and parenting relationships surrounding a defiant teen? I believe it has something to do with the unique role that fathers have within the home. Think of the wording Jesus used when teaching His disciples to pray. He instructed them to refer to God as *our Father.*

Fathers are given the distinctive responsibility of serving as an earthly, physical representation of our heavenly Father—and all that comes with it. A father is to exhibit God's unconditional love, acceptance and grace, and also His holiness, righteousness and sovereignty. When a household lacks a gentle and wise, yet strong and authoritative, father, the family apparently doesn't function as well as it should.

I'm not saying that homes without fathers are in any way doomed to failure. We will talk about the redemptive power of single-parent homes in the next chapter. What I am saying is that when the characteristics of the father figure in the home are exactly opposite of the characteristics of our heavenly Father, then dysfunction ensues. One father of a defiant teen in the study demonstrated this point: "The kids are basically good, so I say, leave them alone."

Confused and Overwhelmed

This characteristic relates to a father's being passive and conflict avoidant, but is slightly different. These dads seem to be—as my own father used to say—"lost as a ginny goose." They seem bewildered, at a complete loss as to how to handle conflict situations with the defiant teen, so they yield almost all of the parental authority to their wives. Their motto seems to be, "When in doubt, clam up and slowly slink away." They're on the lookout for the path of least resistance, a way to make the conflict disappear as quickly as possible.

If you happen to be a history buff, do you know who Neville Chamberlain was? No, he is not the Hall of Fame basketball player made famous by his play with the Lakers, 76ers and Harlem Globetrotters . . . that would *Wilt* Chamberlain. No relation, by the way. Neville Chamberlain was the British prime minister in the late 1930s who put forth a strategy for avoiding war with an increasingly violent and aggressive Germany. He believed that simply giving Adolf Hitler what he wanted—at the time, part of the Czech region—would persuade the power-hungry fiend to be nice and leave England and the rest of Europe alone. Boy, did Chamberlain get that wrong. His failed policy was so infamous it became known—and mocked—throughout history as "peace through appeasement": "I'll give you whatever you want; just leave me alone."

Many dads of defiant teens take this very approach. Confused about what disciplinary course of action to take and overwhelmed by the constant agitation, they just try to make the conflict go away as expeditiously as possible. This approach has failed all throughout world history, and it is destined to fail as a means of achieving peace with defiant teens, as well.

Feel Forced to Engage in the Discipline Process

One husband in the study put it this way: "My wife wants me to be stricter, so I'm stricter. And I look at it like having a job where you're required to comply with company policy. You may not agree with the policy, but nevertheless, you've got to do it." These conflict avoidant dads are not only trying to avoid conflict with their oppositional kids, they are also trying desperately to keep things quiet with the missus. How do they choose to accomplish that? That's right—peace through appeasement. If she wants him to be harder on the kids, he'll do it . . . at least while she's watching. But behind her back, he'll make comments to the defiant child like, "Okay, the warden says you've got to go to your room, so I guess you've got to go."

I believe that the majority of men who accompany their wives to my office to deal with the behavior of a defiant teen are there solely because of their wives. From the looks on their faces, they would rather be chewing glass than discussing their family issues with a counselor. These fathers tend to minimize the problems with their child, downplay the need for intervention and make vain attempts to justify the defiant teen's behavior. Only the persistent insistence of their wives compels them to take seriously the situation at home. And when they feel forced by their wives to make the difficult discipline and parenting choices, their passive-aggressive nature kicks in. They'll comply with the program . . . but inside, they're dragging their feet all the way.

Often Exhibit Delayed Explosiveness

I affectionately call these men "hand grenade dads." They delay dealing with a problem with a defiant child—I mean, they delay and delay and delay—until they finally explode in a frenzy of rage. This angry outburst will not necessarily be aimed at the behavior of the defiant teen, even though he or she would be the expected target. Many times, the detonation is directed at the wife, because he believes that she's the cause of the conflict, or because she's making him look bad in front of the children.

These reasons, which make perfect sense to the hand grenade dad, adequately justify his behavior in his own mind. The first reason he feels justified in throwing a childish temper-tantrum is because he disagrees with how his wife is handling the current discipline situation. For example, he has told her time and time again to back off and not push the kids so much. Since she didn't listen to his plan, he feels completely within his rights to take control of the situation and force her to back off. The second reason this type of dad might explode at his wife is that he's tired of feeling emasculated by her. She has chastised him in front of his kids, told anyone who would listen what a horrible father he is and accused him—whether with words or meaningful looks—of being less than a man for not backing her up against the defiant child. He finally snaps under the weight of frustration, determined to put a stop to her disrespectful behavior. Unfortunately, he has picked the most destructive, devastating and ultimately unhelpful strategy possible.

Common Characteristics of Wives in Homes of Defiant Teens

The wives who participated in the study also shared some common characteristics. As we look at the following behaviors, note how the characteristics exhibited by these mothers of extremely defiant teens seem to mesh naturally with those of their husbands.

Feel Abandoned

Bottom line: These women feel alone. They are forced to deal with all the mayhem in their families while their husbands are at work, and they have to continue handling the problems even after Dad comes home because their husbands refuse to engage. One wife stated, "I feel like I'm on this island all by myself. I'm trying to do what is right and my husband is not behind me on it. He's not backing me up, much less standing beside me, enforcing the discipline with our child."

Their husbands' refusal to engage with the situation means they are completely on their own in combating a child's defiance. They alone are willing to do the hard work and make the tough choices that come with trying to successfully parent an extremely defiant child. They feel unloved and unprotected, betrayed by husbands who leave them to drown when the parenting waters get rough.

For example, I was speaking with a husband and wife who were struggling with a very defiant 17-year-old son. Over the previous weekend, during a particularly explosive episode, things got physically rough. Apparently, the son had refused to comply with his grounding and attempted to leave the house against his mother's orders. When she had tried to stop him, the boy shoved his mom up against the kitchen counter and raised his hand as though to hit her. Now, the husband was in the kitchen as well. How would you guess he dealt with the situation? He grabbed their 10-year-old daughter and took her upstairs so that she wouldn't have to see the conflict. Can you believe that? A six-foot-two man was physically assaulting his wife, and he ran upstairs and left her to face the situation all alone. To say that his wife felt abandoned would be an understatement. I realize that this is an extreme example, but wives feel similarly abandoned by their husbands in parenting situations every day.

Feel Angry with Their Husbands

Almost without exception, these women are mad. They are angry at their husbands for lacking the backbone to stand up to their defiant kids and for failing to come alongside them to provide desperately needed support and assistance. Other reasons these women give for being mad at their husbands include: because he is disengaged, because he has abandoned her to do all the hard parenting work, because she is always forced to be the bad guy, because he ignores the kids—until he explodes with anger at them—and because he acts like he wants to be their child's friend rather than a parent.

Usually, anger is a response to feeling that one has been treated unfairly or has suffered an unjust consequence. In other words, anger generally stems from the feeling of being wronged in some way. These women definitely feel wronged. They believe that the entire burden of parenting has been placed squarely—and quite unfairly—on their shoulders. When they see other husbands and fathers step up to the plate and do their fair share raising their kids, these women feel as though they have lost the spousal lottery, as if the men they married are missing the parenting genes required to take on the added pressure of raising a defiant child.

Express a Sense of Hopelessness

One of the main signs of clinical depression is a general sense of hopelessness about life. This is when a person "globalizes" a negative experience to include all of life. Where others might rightfully recognize a current situation as being really bad, depressed people tend to extrapolate the lack of hope in their present circumstances and apply it to all of life.

One of the most prominent characteristics exhibited by mothers in the midst of raising a defiant child is a sense of hopelessness. One wife put it this way: "My husband told me one time that he was not going to change, that I'm not going to change and that our defiant child isn't going to change, so we just have to muddle through. It's so . . . hopeless."

Does this mean these mothers are clinically depressed? Many most assuredly are and would benefit from seeing their doctor for treatment. But most of these women are, quite simply, overwhelmed by the painful reality of their situation. They see the enormity of their predicament and feel hopeless because they lack the support they need. As we've seen, many of these women receive little assistance from their husbands in dealing with the defiant child. To make things worse, their families of origin tend to be more judgmental than helpful, and they are too ashamed of their circumstance to seek help from friends or extended family.

A sense of isolation, and the hopelessness that accompanies it, is one of the most devastating and insidious effects of parenting a defiant teen. You can hear the desperation in the voice of this wife and mother: "I mean, it's just a world of criticism, hate and guilt. And you just . . . there's nothing good about it . . . nothing."

Feel Like Bad Parents

A common point of concern for many of these women is a doubt in their own abilities as mother and wives. One wife said, "Have we done something to inadvertently cause this in our child? Was it our parenting methods?" Every time they see a happy family at church or at the park or a restaurant, these women tend to suffer agonizing guilt over the present state of their family. In the aftermath of so many ugly episodes in their home, their minds race back to all the "what ifs" and "if onlys" of their past years of parenting. What if they had been stricter? If only they would have been more consistent! One mother in the study identified the source of her guilt: "I feel like I've failed as a parent. I feel like that if he's acting like this, then it's because of our upbringing of him."

This self-doubt contributes to a mother's feelings of depression and hopelessness. Compounding the situation is that many mothers, as discussed earlier, allow their guilt over previous parenting mistakes to influence their current parenting decisions. They feel so bad about how they or their spouse conducted themselves in the past that they fail to hold the line and make the difficult parenting decisions needed in the present. They feel as if they need to somehow "make up" for the sins of the past. Of course, this line of thinking only perpetuates the poor parenting choices, and therefore perpetuates a continuing sense of guilt.

The Impact on the Marriage Relationship

Do all husbands and wives who are parenting an extremely defiant teen share these characteristics? Of course not. But the research does indicate that such behaviors are common within this population. The participants in the study were not picked because of the severity of their cases but because they represented the average couple parenting a defiant child.

Did you recognize yourself or your spouse in any of these descriptions? If so, I hope you'll take heart in knowing that you are not alone in your experience. Many Christian couples are going through the exact same thing. If you saw yourself in any of those characteristics, you'll want to pay particularly close attention as we look at how they can lead to negative results in your marriage relationship and how disaster can be averted before it happens.

As we discussed in the beginning of the book, the home of a defiant child is full of trauma, bitterness, arguing, tension, and constant turmoil. A marriage enduring that level of stress over a prolonged period of time cannot help but be impacted. In my experience, when a couple comes in with a defiant teen and yet has a marriage relationship in tip-top condition, it is the exception to the rule.

Most marriages are like a balloon: You can't see any holes until you fill it with water. Then, the pressure of the water quickly reveals the hidden weak spots. In a marriage, you generally can't see the weak spots until pressure is applied. Parenting a defiant child over several long months or years is certainly pressure enough to test the limits of even the strongest marriages.

Let's look at four of the most common indicators that a marriage relationship has been strained to the breaking point by the presence of a defiant teen.

Bipolar Parenting

Bipolar parenting occurs when each spouse stakes out territory at polar-opposite ends of the discipline spectrum. Each feels that it is their duty to countermand the harmful parenting choices of the other and bring balance back to the family.

Larry and Alice perfectly illustrate this phenomenon. As we sat talking in my office, Larry said, "With my wife, it's like living with Hitler. Alice is just on the kids constantly. She never lets up. Somebody has got to loosen things up a little and show some grace. That's what I do."

Alice responded, "Grace!? Larry doesn't show grace. He doesn't show any boundaries at all. It's like I have another child in the house. If it were left up to him, these kids would run wild. I'm the only one trying to make these kids do what is right."

Many parents don't necessarily agree with each other all the time about how best to raise their children; differing views about the best or most effective discipline choice commonly provoke disagreements in marriage. But most couples are able to hash out these differences, come to some form of compromise and continue on together in the parenting process. Couples who quarrel about how best to discipline an extremely defiant child, however, are often unable to resolve their parental disagreements quite so easily. They lose sight of the fact that they are on the same team, and develop more of an adversarial relationship. One wife from the study stated, "As our defiant child got older, my husband started having opinions on how to handle him, and I didn't agree with those. That's what caused this huge conflict."

Bipolar parents see each other as the enemy and form a triangulated relationship with the defiant child. They do not present a united front to the child. And they are not simply divided; they have become bitter rivals who are constantly antagonistic toward one another. As one of the husbands in the study put it: "I think a lot of it has to do with what we brought into the marriage. How we were parented. Because some of the things she really wants me to be serious about are not ingrained in me that way. She has a big problem with that."

Breakdown in Communication

Way back in the early days of coalmining, it was a common practice to bring a caged canary into the mine. Why? Well, it wasn't to keep the miners company or to allow them the opportunity to teach the bird the latest drinking song. No, canaries just happen to be very sensitive to gases such as methane or carbon monoxide that could leak into the mine and be harmful to the miners. The sophisticated ventilation systems used today had not yet been invented, so the noble canary served as the early warning system of dangerous gas buildup. If the little bird was perky and chirping, then the air was okay, but if the miners saw an unmoving lump of feathers at the bottom of the cage, they knew it was time to get out of the mine as fast as they could.

A breakdown in communication often serves as the "canary in the coalmine" for a marriage relationship. It is the early warning system that signals the approach of more serious or even deadly relational issues. You've probably been in a restaurant and noticed another couple who must be mad at each other. What's your first clue? They're not speaking. Communication is one of the first relational components to stop working when the marital bond is under strain.

Communication provides an intimate connection between a husband and a wife, something that transcends anything physical or practical. Communication serves as the lifeline that joins one human being with the other in a meaningful relationship. When that relationship is clogged with stress, communication becomes a difficult and laborious task.

Couples tend to stop talking with each other for one of two reasons: *fear* or *frustration*. If we fear the response of our spouse, we just won't bring up or discuss the potentially problematic issue. And if frustration has built up because we've had the same conversation 10 million times and the other person never changes, we won't be interested in rehashing the subject yet again.

The tough parenting and discipline decisions related to dealing with an extremely defiant child provide ample opportunity for a couple to accumulate feelings of fear and frustration. Because one spouse fears the other's response or is frustrated by the other's inability to see the situation his or her way, that spouse chooses to stay quiet. And when communication remains cut off for a long period of time, this breakdown can drastically affect the overall health, and even the survival, of the relationship.

Blaming the Other Spouse

One wife participating in the study said, "I would be furious with my child about something fairly minor and I'd realize in the midst of it that I was more furious with my husband for what he did than I was at the child for what he did."

Parental disagreements over discipline choices can escalate rapidly into arguments and finger-pointing. Just to be clear: *Disagreement* is not the same as *argument*. In a disagreement, the parties are attempting to solve a problem. They are open to discussing various options for resolving their difference of opinion. An argument, however, is personal. It's about winning, about power and about being right. Couples tell me all the time, "We had a big blowup over the weekend, but you know, I can't remember what it was about." That's because the originating issue is one of the first casualties of the conflict. The dispute quickly turns from being about solving a problem to inflicting emotional pain on the adversary.

The discipline disagreements between some husbands and wives who are parenting extremely defiant kids can turn into one long, ongoing argument over who's right and who's wrong. Every time a crisis occurs, each spouse points to the other as the primary culprit. Rather than discussing the child's behavior as a problem to be solved by two people who love each other and have overcome countless problems in the past, the couple turns their conversation into an accusation-filled dispute that never gets resolved. Instead of focusing on how to guide the defiant child toward better choices, each blames the other for putting the "dys-" in their dysfunctional family.

Overall Weakening of the Marriage Relationship

The fourth indicator that a marriage has been strained to the limit by the presence of a defiant child probably won't come as a surprise. Let's recap what we've observed so far about these relationships:

- We have husbands who just want to be left alone, and who feel bitter toward their wives for forcing them to do things they don't want to do and at times making them feel emasculated.

- We have wives who feel abandoned, angry, hopeless and guilty.

- We have marriage relationships in which each spouse is pitted against the other in bitter parenting warfare, each blaming the other for the negative state of their families, neither wanting to even talk with the other anymore about their problems.

I would say that these marriages have been significantly weakened throughout the ordeal of parenting an extremely defiant child.

This is, of course, the goal of the Evil One. His plan from the start has been to destroy any Christian home that he can get his hands on, and using the disruption that comes with raising an extremely defiant child is as good a way as any. Scripture reminds us in 1 Peter 5:8, "Be self-controlled and alert. Your enemy the devil prowls around like a roaring lion looking for someone to devour." He wants more than anything else to devour you and your marriage, so if you allow the tension in your home to create sizable cracks in your marriage relationship, you're playing right into the Adversary's hands.

Almost all of us were charged during our marriage ceremonies with these words of Jesus: "'For this reason a man will leave his father and mother and be united to his wife, and the two will become one flesh.' So they are no longer two, but one. Therefore what God has joined together, let man not separate" (Matt. 19:5-6). Do you still believe that Jesus was being straight with us there? Has truth changed since you walked down the aisle? Of course Jesus was telling the truth, and His words remain true. God joined you together with your spouse; your marriage was a holy and God-ordained event. So, your spouse may be a lot of things, but he is not your enemy. Your spouse may have a lot of flaws, but she is not your adversary.

If you believe the Enemy's lie that your spouse is to blame for your family's unrest, then he has succeeded in distracting you from the real battle. We need to be reminded again of Paul's words in Ephesians 6:12: "For our struggle is not against flesh and blood, but against the rulers, against the authorities, against the powers of this dark world and against the spiritual forces of evil in the heavenly realms."

As I mentioned at the beginning of this book, your defiant child is not your enemy—and neither is your spouse, no matter how miserable a parent he or she may be. If you're going to get mad at somebody, get mad at the true source of all the heartache in your family: the father of lies, the deceiver, your old foe, the devil.

Fixing the Problems Before They Happen

Now that we've looked at how parenting an oppositional/defiant child can negatively impact a marriage, we need to ask the obvious question: Are these consequences inevitable? Are parents of defiant teens helplessly tied to a railroad track, doomed to watch the slow train of marital destruction bear down on them? Absolutely not.

The first step in resolving any problem is to realize that you have one. Simply knowing that the potential exists for these issues to arise in your marriage, or recognizing that they exist now, is crucial to preventing severe damage to your marriage relationship. So let's consider some strategies that can help you avoid or eliminate each of these problems.

How to Avoid Bipolar Parenting

We've already discussed the best way to keep parents on the same page and help them come to an agreement on parenting boundaries and consequences. Do you remember what it was? The behavior contract. Again, in my mind, this is the absolute best way to avoid bipolar parenting. Why does it work?

- **A contract forces compromise.** When disagreements arise between two people who love each other, compromise is in order. A willingness to compromise shows that you value partner, your partner's ideas and your relationship, and that you realize you do not have a monopoly on the truth. In working toward a compromise on the contract, couples must remember that agreement and unity are one million times more important than either of you being right. If a couple can work together to reach a compromise on the boundaries and consequences in a contract, then half the battle against bipolar parenting already has been won.

- **A contract takes away individual discipline choices.** A contract enables the parents to speak with one voice. Once a contract is in place, it doesn't matter which parent implements the consequence. One parent is not going to be more lenient or harsh than the other. This removes the teen's motivation to pit one parent against the other.

- **A contract abolishes good guy/bad guy roles.** The driving force behind bipolar parenting is the desire to offset the destructive parenting choices of the other parent. With a contract, that need is sent packing, because both parents are acting in unison. There ain't no good guys and there ain't no bad guys; there's only you and me, and we just . . . sorry! I just had a '70s flashback. But you get my drift.

- **A contract demonstrates parental unity to the defiant child.** As we've mentioned before, the greatest gift you can give your children is a strong, stable marriage. To have their parents warring with each other is extremely unsettling for all the children in the house, and that instability can become yet another catalyst driving the defiant child's negative behavior. When you show a rebellious child that he does not possess the power to come between you and your beloved, you send a strong and powerful message. He would never admit it, but he finds it reassuring to know that his parents' love for each other is an immovable constant in his life.

If you recognize bipolar parenting creeping into your household, I urge you to run—don't walk!—to formulate a contract today.

How to Avoid a Breakdown in Communication

What happens if, one day, you notice an unmoving lump of feathers at the bottom of the canary cage of your marriage? It's sad that the little thing choked to death on the negative feelings that built up in your relationship, but there's still time to get some fresh air and save your marriage. I have two suggestions for repairing—or avoiding—the kind of communication problems that signal the slow slide into relationship failure. One is an overarching philosophy and the other is a useful little tool.

First, never stop talking with each other—*never!* If you talk with a professional hostage or union or trade negotiator, you'll hear this advice: Keep the other party talking. As long as the parties continue talking, there's a chance to work things out. But when talking ceases, the opportunity for a breakthrough all but disappears.

This is one of the Adversary's most powerful weapons against a married couple: "You've been hurt. You've been treated poorly," he whispers. And the wounded partner thinks, *My spouse doesn't deserve communication with me. My spouse deserves to know just how poorly she has treated me.* I think I can speak for all of us when I say that I'm very glad Jesus doesn't take that point of view with us. I'm so grateful that no matter what I do or how badly I treat Him, His arms are always open wide and His ears are always open.

This is why "keep talking" should be an overarching, guiding principle in any marriage. No matter how mad we are, no matter how unfairly we've been treated, no matter how hurtful the words or actions of our supposed "loved one," we will never stop talking to each other. We may take a short break to calm down and let the adrenaline subside, but we will always keep the lines of communication open, no matter what. Regardless how serious the problem or how hopeless the situation may seem, if you keep talking, the possibility of reconciliation is always present.

My second piece of advice is this: VALUE your partner during a problem-solving discussion. VALUE is an acrostic, a handy little tool that many couples find useful in regulating their communication and steering their conversations in helpful directions. It helps a couple . . .

- Avoid a harsh beginning that leads to an anger-filled argument
- Be sure each spouse actually listens to the other and hears what is said
- Focus the discussion on problem-solving negotiation, not winning a power struggle
- Remember always the unconditional love that God has placed between them
- See the conflict through the eyes of their spouse and gain a unique perspective

Validate Your Partner at the Start of a Problem-solving Discussion
This simply means acknowledging that your partner has a valid point of view. He or she isn't stupid, brain-dead or crazy. Another random

person presented with the same information could very well come to the same conclusion your partner has reached. In practice, this means resisting the temptation to say, "What kind of idiot thinks that it's okay to watch a football game while his wife is out mowing the lawn?!" and saying instead, "I understand how important that game is to you, but we agreed to get the yard work done first." Validating your spouse's perspective sets the stage for problem-solving, instead of tearing down the stage with an argument.

Actively Listen to Your Spouse
By active listening, I mean a focused, purposeful, intentional attempt to listen to what your spouse is saying and hear the meaning of his or her words. If we're honest, in an argument most of us are only listening for our spouse to take a breath so that we can jump in and throw another verbal punch. Active listening is characterized by repeating back to your partner, verbatim, the words that come out of his or her mouth, until the speaking spouse agrees that the listening spouse got it right. Many couples find this much more difficult than it sounds, but the payoff is worth the effort. When you actively listen, you ultimately may still disagree, but your spouse cannot say that you didn't listen to his or her point of view.

Lose to Win
In other words, be more concerned with finding resolution and initiating reconciliation than with being right. Ninety percent of marital disagreements can be negotiated down to an agreed-upon resolution or put to rest with a simple apology. Proving your spouse to be wrong may prove you right, but you will be right for all the wrong reasons. Jesus said, "What good will it be for a man if he gains the whole world, yet forfeits his soul?" (Matt. 16:26). The same principle applies here. What good does it do for you to be found right and your spouse wrong if in the end you damage—or lose—the marriage relationship? By losing to win, you enter the problem-solving discussion with a priority of resolving the conflict, recognizing that you must be willing to give up something on your end to accomplish that purpose.

Unconditional Love Must Guide Your Interactions
Whenever a couple disagrees, their love for each other and commitment to each other should never be in question. The heavenly Father united married couples in love. That love is unconditional, and the couple's interactions should always reflect that. This means the word "divorce" has to be removed from the vocabulary of the disagreeing couple. The *D*-word is too easy and dangerous a weapon for a spouse to wield during a heated conflict. If every time a couple has a dust-up, one of the spouses threatens divorce, then all communication, compromise and reconciliation come to an end. The *D*-word becomes a threat meant to intimidate and control.

If you have two cats that don't get along and you close them up together in a small closet, those two cats are going to have to work things out! I'm not advocating animal cruelty; just illustrating a point. You see the same concept played out in business and labor negotiations. During "locked door" sessions, the two negotiating parties are not allowed to leave the room. When leaving is not an option, you are forced to work things out and come to a resolution.

If a couple leaves divorce, or the threat of divorce, off the table, then they are forced to come to a resolution. They know they're going to be together in this marriage and parenting thing for the rest of their lives, so they have no choice but to come to an agreement.

Empathy Leads to New Perspective
One of the most valuable skills you can practice as a mature Christian adult is the art of empathy. As you know, *empathy* basically means viewing something from someone else's point of view—feeling their pain, so to speak. This skill is critical for married couples.

Early in our marriage, I had a fight—er, I mean, I had a problem-solving discussion—with Beth. I got frustrated and left the house to go to Home Depot or something to cool off. On the way back home, I had one of those ball-peen hammer experiences with God. You know, one of those moments when it feels like God reaches down and pops you right between the eyes with a ball-peen hammer. He reminded me that, frustrated as I was with Beth, living with me was no piece of cake, either.

God opened my eyes to my faults and shortcomings and helped me see the wisdom in extracting the giant sequoia redwood tree from my own eye before I tried to take the little splinter out of Beth's. Ever since that epiphany, I've tried to remember to see things from her perspective whenever we have a disagreement. I don't always succeed, but that's my goal. Practicing empathy is key in squelching anger and promoting reconciliation.

How to Avoid Blame and Overall Weakening of the Marriage Relationship

All the issues that contribute to marital discord—anger, jealousy, frustration, guilt, bitterness, unforgiveness, detachment, accusation and dishonesty, just to name a few—generally are surface issues that point back to a root problem. I believe that, in a vast majority of cases, that root problem is a spiritual one.

Although our primary focus at The Timothy Center is on working with adolescents, we work with all other age groups as well. Over the years, I've counseled a large number of married couples who were struggling in their relationships. In my experience, not one of those couples, in all that time, was growing and maturing in their faith.

Couples with severe marital problems are couples with spiritual problems. A couple who is spiritually grounded in their faith will, of course, still have problems, but they are able to work through those problems productively, with grace and forgiveness. I always tell couples that their relationship with their spouse mirrors their relationship with God. If one is distant and detached, most likely the other will be as well, because those two relationships are intricately intertwined.

This means that we need to seek spiritual solutions to relational problems before we try other routes. As I stated earlier, I have found Matthew 6:33 to be one of the most useful truths from God's Word for the families I work with. This is certainly true for struggling couples. When you feel as though your marriage and your world are crumbling down around you, seek first the kingdom of God and His righteousness. Then you will find peace in entrusting to God all the problems within your family, remembering that you don't carry this burden alone. This is a promise from the Creator of the universe. He promises us that when we seek Him with all our hearts, we will find Him—and in that intimate relationship, we will find a peace that surpasses all human understanding. In your marriage, the answer is not to give up and bail out; it is to seek God and surrender to His will.

I know that telling you to "pray about it" may come across as trite or clichéd, but I just happen to believe that it's the absolute best choice you can make. No amount of time spent in communication training or in figuring out which of you is from Mars and which is from Venus can heal the deep, hurtful wounds so many couples have. So instead of standing up to your misguided spouse and pointing out each and every flaw, I suggest that you kneel down before your Savior and seek His forgiveness and reconciliation. My experience and my Bible tell me that you will receive the healing you need only from a touch of the Master's hand.

To Sum It Up

In this chapter, we discussed some of the characteristics commonly exhibited by husbands and wives who are parenting an extremely defiant child. We looked at how those characteristics can lead to negative behaviors within the marriage relationship, including bipolar parenting, a breakdown in communication, blaming the other spouse for the family's problems and an overall weakening of the marital relationship. We also examined strategies for counteracting these negative effects, including:

- Implementing a contract as a way to avoid the trap of bipolar parenting

- VALUEing your spouse during problem-solving discussions to avoid a breakdown in communication

- Pursuing a healthy spiritual life to protect your marriage against the temptation to blame, to strengthen your relationship for the constant stress and strain of parenting a defiant child, and to gain the peace and healing your heart longs for.

A Quick Follow-up

We began this chapter by looking the troubled marriage of Bill and Lilly. They were at odds with each other over how each handled the disciplinary responsibilities for their defiant child. In situations like this, the trouble with the child is usually a surface problem pointing to a root cause. The root cause in this situation was a trouble marriage that was being exacerbated by the behavior of the defiant child. I recommended that the couple seek marital counseling from one of my associates, and they agreed to go. I was encouraged to learn from Bill and Lilly at a later date just how successful their therapy had been. This couple was talking to each other more and yelling at each other less. They were seeing each other as allies and no longer as enemies. They became a united front when it came to parenting their defiant child, and once he became re-acclimated to the new relational structure in his home, he also improved in his rebellious behavior. The family still had to work through many issues, but the road to reconciliation was paved by a healed marriage.

HAVE A SEAT ON THE COUCH

1. Did any of the common characteristics of the husbands and wives in the study reflect behaviors you've observed in yourself or your spouse? If so, explain how.

2. Which, if any, of the negative effects of parenting a defiant child have already impacted your marriage? What evidence have you seen that suggests this is a problem?

3. Do you believe using the VALUE acrostic is a practical way to avoid some of the common communication problems with married couples? Why or why not? Do you think it could be useful for you? Why or why not?

4. List some practical ways a couple could get their spiritual relationship back on track.

5. Do you think your spouse would be willing to pray with you about your family's situation and your marriage relationship? Why? Why not? What's keeping you from asking right now?

10

SPECIAL FOCUS: SINGLE-PARENT AND BLENDED FAMILIES

As you have learned, either from experience or from reading this book, parenting an exceptionally defiant teenager is one of the most difficult and demanding tasks any parent can undertake. Successfully navigating the treacherous waters of teenage opposition is extremely challenging under the best of conditions. Even when the parents' marriage is intact and their relationship is solid, the tension and stress related to raising an oppositional child has pushed many "typical" nuclear families to the breaking point.

In single-parent families and blended families, the challenges of dealing with an overly rebellious child are complicated by special circumstances and seemingly unrelated problems. Parents in these situations—without the ability to share the load with the child's other parent—often feel as if they're at a distinct disadvantage and have to work twice as hard to get the job done. It's like being required to compete in an Iron Man Triathlon while wearing 30-pound ankle weights.

Only the men, women and children involved can truly appreciate the amount of pain, confusion and turmoil that accompanies the end of a marriage. These families desperately need Christian friends and family who will wrap their arms around them, love them and give them the support they need to stand strong.

If you have gone through or are going through a painful transition like this, let me reassure you that your family doesn't have to match a particular design to earn God's blessing. If you will let Him, your heavenly Father still deeply desires to be right in the middle of your present circumstance, whatever shape your family takes. Regardless of whether you are a single parent or have created a blended family through remarriage, God is still watching over you with love, and His promise to work all things together for your ultimate good still stands (see Rom. 8:28).

However, your situation deserves special attention as you determine how to most effectively parent your defiant teen. Let's begin by examining the special difficulties faced by single parents in trying to raise a rebellious child.

Unique Challenges for the Single-Parent Home

Single-parent homes are an ever-increasing segment of the family landscape in our country. Before 1970, one out of every ten homes in America was led by a single parent; by the turn of the twenty-first century, that number had grown to one in every three families.[1] One in three! That amazing statistic confirms, if this is the situation in your home, that your family is not on the fringes of society, but that you are joined by a significant portion of both the general population and America's church family.

Single parents face a number of issues specifically related to the breakup of a marriage and the redefinition of the family:

- They must come to grips with the loss of their marriage.
- They have to wrap their brains around the new role they are forced to play and all the new responsibilities they face.
- They have to redefine all their relationships with their family and friends.
- They need to create a new working relationship with their ex-spouse for the good of their children.[2]

Although these challenges confront every new single parent, single moms have to clear even more hurdles. Mothers are given primary custody 85 to 90 percent of the time.[3] Even though these numbers have begun to shift in recent years, with more single fathers taking custodial responsibility, moms still make up the vast majority of parents trying to raise their kids alone.

These moms face an appalling array of obstacles to successfully raising their kids, and finances pose one of the biggest challenges. Women,
as a whole, still do not receive equivalent compensation for equivalent
work, so they are at a financial disadvantage from the outset. Many are
forced to work longer hours, take extra shifts or find second jobs just to
barely make ends meet. By contrast, custodial fathers receive, on average, twice the financial income of their ex-wives.[4] *But*, you say, *aren't these
mothers more than compensated by the child support fathers are required to pay?*
Good question, but the fact is that within the first couple of years, 70
percent of noncustodial fathers become delinquent in their child support payments.[5] The energy it takes a mom in this situation to simply
ensure her family's survival leaves little left over to deal with the hard-
ships associated with raising a defiant child on her own.

Let's examine some of the specific struggles facing single parents of
extremely oppositional teens.

Isolation

Parenting an oppositional teen requires a philosophy of all-hands-on-
deck. It forces both parents to work together, focus on the issues and
confront the problems from a united front in order to take advantage
of the power in numbers. Solomon pointed out in Ecclesiastes 4:12,
"Though one may be overpowered, two can defend themselves. A cord
of three strands is not quickly broken." Few single parents have access
to the strength and comfort of sharing their burden with a partner. As
a result, many struggle with a sense of isolation. They feel alone because
they *are* alone.

When a defiant teen pulls yet another stunt late at night when you
are thoroughly exhausted, there is no one else to take care of the problem. When the principal demands a meeting about your child's disruption at school . . . and when someone needs to accompany him to court
for his speeding ticket day after tomorrow . . . and when he needs a ride
to football practice because he's grounded from driving—you have to
do it all. The single parent has to make every trip and take off all that
time from work because no one else is available to help shoulder some
of this gigantic load.

Gone are the days when most of us lived within a couple of blocks of all our siblings, parents and extended family, who stood ready to help out a family member in need. The transient nature of our society also means that few of us enjoy longstanding, deep relationships with neighbors who can lend a helping hand in times of trouble. So the single parent of a defiant teen feels isolated, forced to face each trial and tribulation unaided.

Lack of Support

Many of the single parents I work with desperately need someone reliable with whom to consult when they face decisions about dealing with a defiant child. The single mom of a defiant 14-year-old called me one day. "This morning I found a baggie of what I'm pretty sure is marijuana on his dresser," she explained. "What should I do?" In a similar situation, the first thing a married parent would do is call her spouse so that they could put their heads together and formulate a plan of action. Many single parents don't have that option; they are left to make every decision and tackle every discipline incident by themselves. This leaves them wondering whether their discipline decisions are correct or whether, as their defiant child claims, they are just plain crazy and stricter than any other parent in the world. These moms and dads aren't shirking their duty; they'd simply feel more confident if they could bounce their decisions off someone else. But very few people know the situation or understand what it's like to parent an extremely rebellious child.

In addition to making these hard decisions on their own, a lack of support means that these parents don't have someone who will encourage them, defend their decisions and help carry out the plan. No one "has their back," so to speak, and the resulting sense of being deserted is palpable. What these parents wouldn't give to have a partner to stand alongside them when they have to take on a teenager who is angry, explosive and out of control.

The Ex-Factor

As difficult as it is to suffer the isolation and lack of support that comes with parenting without a partner, many single parents have the added complication of an ex-spouse who actively works against their parenting strategy and undermines them at every turn. These parents are constantly embroiled in conflict over discipline choices, battling not only their defiant child but their ex-spouse, as well.

Every day, I see ex-spouses at war with each other over every little issue regarding their kids. One particular mother, who seemed well-balanced and was clearly trying to do the right thing for her kids, described to me the constant conflict with her former spouse. Because every phone call degenerated into a screaming match, they had resorted to sending scathing emails back and forth in an attempt to communicate with each other about the children. She described—and her child confirmed the story—how her ex told her children that she was nuts, that they didn't have to obey her and that he would never have those kind of rules if they chose to come and live with him.

This sad scenario plays out in countless homes across this country every day. And do you know what I find even more tragic? This accurately describes many Christian homes as well. I have witnessed some of the most bitter and vindictive actions come from ex-spouses who claim to be believers. In fact, many are so confused that they truly believe that their harmful actions are spiritually justified. They're convinced they are "fighting the good fight" on behalf of their children, and that Jesus would be pleased with their actions. In the misguided belief that they are "on God's side," people take license to do some of the most ungodly things. And as you might guess, this continual stream of parental conflict is like a constant flow of gasoline on the fire of a child's defiant behavior.

Solutions for Single Parents

Although the additional challenges you face as a single parent may tempt you to give up, I want to share some good news: You can take specific steps to overcome these hurdles and return a measure of peace and hope to your household.

Avoiding Isolation and Finding Support
As John Donne once wrote, "No man is an island, entire of itself . . ." Now, you might be an isthmus, or maybe even a peninsula, but nobody

is an island. Simply put: We need each other. None of us was created to function on our own, separate from the rest of humanity.

I encourage all single parents with defiant children to do whatever it takes to find support and social interaction. I know that this may sound unrealistic, given your schedule and all the extra turmoil that comes with having an oppositional teen, but it is absolutely vital that you make that connection with someone. Like many of my clients, you may be hearing a little voice inside of you saying that no one can help because no one will ever understand. Or maybe that voice is discouraging you from opening up to anyone because they would only judge you and push you away, leaving you more alone than ever. Let me encourage you to listen to that voice closely so that you can recognize it in the future. That voice you hear is the Evil One, weaving his web of devastating lies in the hopes of convincing you to remain isolated and alone. You're a much more attractive victim that way.

Now, listen closely to the truth: Most people will understand and be supportive, if you will just give them a chance. Based on my experience with hundreds of parents in similar situations, I am convinced that there are people in your life right now who would treasure the opportunity to love you and help you when times get rough, or to simply provide a shoulder to lean on. Don't be too afraid or too proud to ask for assistance. Call a family member and ask if he would be willing to let you bounce some discipline ideas off of him. Think of someone at work who might have some helpful insight or a different perspective to share on parenting matters. Ask a member of your church if she would be willing to watch your kids to give you some time off. Look for parent groups in your area, perhaps connected to your church or your child's school district.

No matter what the Enemy says, you will not be a burden and you will not be overstepping your bounds. Remember: God has placed certain people in your life for a reason. You simply need to identify those who are ready, able and willing to help. The bottom line is this: Wherever you go and however you do it, find an outlet, a listening ear, a voice of wisdom, a friend. We all need them, and for a single parent with a defiant child, a support team is an absolute necessity.

One other note: Don't ask your child to meet your emotional needs. This is a huge pitfall of single parenting, and it can be devastating for a child. When a mother complains to her 14-year-old daughter about the trouble her father is causing or confides in her 16-year-old son her desperation over meeting financial responsibilities that month, Mom may feel better afterward, but her children will suffer under the weight of the emotional burden she has inappropriately shared. This type of emotional intimacy causes serious deterioration in the parent-child relationship. Yes, you need someplace to vent and get things off your chest; that's just another reason to find an adult friend or confidant to share those things with. Let your children be your children, and don't ask them to shoulder your adult burdens.

Dealing with the Ex

Attempting to coordinate with an ex-spouse concerning parenting issues can be one of the most frustrating and infuriating experiences connected with divorce. Two people who don't get along very well are inescapably tied to each other forever by the parenting responsibilities for their children. So let's consider how to make the best of this difficult situation.

First of all, many divorced parents are able to make a priority of presenting a united front to their children despite their differences. This is a mother and father who have decided to put the welfare of their children above petty unforgiveness or past resentment. This is a mother and father who love their kids more than they dislike each other. We all know divorce can be one of the most devastating events in the life of a child. However, if the parents can manage to get along during the process, encourage an ongoing relationship between the children and both parents and focus on their agreement about parenting rather than their past disagreements with each other, that impact can be greatly diminished.[6]

Continuity and *stability* are the keys to minimizing the negative effects of divorce in the life of a child. If the two ex-spouses generally agree about proper boundaries and consequences, then making sure that those rules and consequences are enforced at both homes can help create that much-needed stability and continuity. This is especially true when an extremely defiant child is involved. I believe that there is a wonderful way to achieve continuity in discipline. I realize I'm beginning to sound like a broken record, but here goes: Institute a behavioral contract. This technique fits the need of this situation to a tee. If parents can agree on a contract and make sure that the contract is the law of the land at both the mother's and the father's homes, then you can achieve the stability and cohesiveness that is so reassuring to kids. Establishing common expectations and consequences also prevents a defiant child from exploiting different parenting styles between the two homes, and thwarts his attempt to pit the parents against each other.

Of course, given the rancor that exists between many divorced couples, this scenario just isn't realistic for some parents. If this is true for you and your former spouse, get your pen and paper out, because I'm about to tell what you can do to convince your ex to agree with your priorities in the parenting department. Are you ready? Here's what you can do: *nothing*. This is sad news, but it is also a fact. One of the most painful but unchangeable consequences of divorce is having your child be influenced by your ex-spouse—along with his or her new spouse, in some cases.

As strongly as you may disagree with how your ex handles discipline, schoolwork, household responsibility, supervision away from home and issues related faith and church, you are fighting a losing battle if you think that you can change his or her parenting philosophy. As devastating as it may be to let your children spend a significant portion of their lives in an environment that you believe is unhealthy, your influence in the affairs of your ex is over. It's time to literally let go and let God. You must trust that your heavenly Father will watch over your children when you cannot. Whenever your kids are away from you, use the opportunity to make them the constant focus of your prayers and petitions before God.

God loves your babies even more than you do, and He considers their welfare a top priority. This is why Jesus gave such a stern warning in Matthew 18:5-6: "And whoever welcomes a little child like this in my name welcomes me. But if anyone causes one of these little ones who believe in me to sin, it would be better for him to have a large millstone hung around his neck and to be drowned in the depths of the sea." God cares for your children. You can trust Him to protect and guide them when they are not under your influence. Leave your kids and your ex to Him, and concentrate instead on what you *can* control.

In short, concentrate on yourself, the only person over whom you have control. Invest your energies not in worrying about your ex-spouse's choices but in carefully examining what you do as a parent and how you do it, to make sure that you are doing right by your kids and in sight of God. In addition to being the *only* thing you can do, it is the absolute *best* thing you can do.

During the times your kids are in your hands, make sure that you lead them, mold them and instruct them in the way that they should go. When they are out of your hands, remember that your heavenly Father still holds them in His loving grasp. And that is the safest place they could possibly be.

Unique Challenges in the Blended Family Home

Parents in blended families also deal with some particular issues that deserve serious consideration. "Stepfamilies," as they are often labeled, account for a large number of American households, and so the challenges they face have a notable effect on our society. Noted family expert Paul Glick has said, "It would not be unreasonable to expect that more than half of all Americans alive today have been, are now, or will eventually be in one or more step situations before they die."[7]

The good news for the stepparent is that you are not alone; unlike the single parent, you have a partner to lean on, confer with and glean support from. But the bad news is that you are not alone. In many cases, you're dealing with a house full of other people who complicate marital and parenting issues to no end. The stress felt by blended families can be just as significant as that of single-parent families, but for different reasons.

There are, of course, two kinds of stepfamilies: those with a stepfather and those with a stepmother. Families with stepfathers seem to experience less stress.[8] This could be attributed to several factors, but the most likely reason is that, in the vast majority of case, mothers retain primary custody of their children. And because mothers tend to take on the primary child-rearing role both before and after divorce, this makes for an easier transition when a stepfather joins the family. Stepmother families, by contrast, tend to have higher stress levels, with significantly higher levels of stress reported by the female children in those families.[9]

The complicated transition of adding a new parent to the family unit can be compared to trying to integrate two entirely different cultures. New rules, new histories, new priorities, new traditions, new boundaries, new expectations and even a whole new family language have to be accepted, learned and applied.

This family transition involves several stages. Early on, during times of family conflict, the group will split along family-of-origin lines, but gradually relationship changes occur and the separateness begins to decrease. In the middle stages of stepfamily transition, the tension builds to a climax. This is when many remarried couples divorce, because, for whatever reasons, they are not willing to work through the heightened relational issues. It can take as long as five to six years for a couple to fully integrate and form a solid couple bond. In the final stages of transition, the relationship between stepparent and stepchildren are strengthened as they finally achieve a stable family attachment.[10]

No matter what type of stepfamily you have, what particular stressors you might experience or what stage of development your family currently is in, adding an extremely defiant child into the mix creates a volatile concoction that can potentially lead to a stepfamily explosion.

Let's examine the particular issues that complicate the process of parenting a defiant teen within a blended family.

His and Hers

One of the first and most difficult tasks of blending a family involves finding healthy ways to share parenting responsibilities. Just today, I met with a couple in my office. Theirs is the second marriage for both

Amy and Jason. She didn't bring any children into the marriage seven years ago, but he is the father of two boys, now ages 18 and 14. The couple also has two younger children together.

The 18-year-old has now moved out of the house to live with his girlfriend. For years, however, his defiant behavior had been a constant source of turmoil in their marriage—and now the 14-year-old is showing similar signs of rebellion. Amy demonstrated the typical response of the wife in a defiant teen's home: She is trying to discipline correctly but feels that her husband had abandoned her, putting her always in the role of the bad guy. Jason, a classic conflict avoider, feels that Amy is way too strict with the kids. One of the first things out of Amy's mouth today was, "I have had it with *your* kids. I am done trying to clean up *your* mess. You can just deal with them from now on. Do you hear me? They're *your* kids and *you* can deal with them *yourself.*"

The frustration Amy feels is certainly understandable, but her reaction highlights one of the major problems exhibited by parents in blended families: a failure to integrate. The old family lines remain drawn and parenting responsibilities remain divided. No matter how aggravated a parent may be, making a distinction between *his* and *hers* causes untold damage.

Stepfamilies split along the lines of *his* and *hers* when one or both parents feel that the biological parent should take the lead, or in some cases full responsibility, in making parenting and discipline decisions for each child. This will prove to be an unsuccessful strategy, especially with a more defiant child. When family differences are emphasized and the parenting responsibilities are split rather than shared, it becomes much more difficult for a blended family to actually blend.

Different Parenting Styles

Many couples fail to discuss their parenting views in depth prior to marriage. They both love kids, they both seem to make practical parenting decisions, so they assume that parenting conflicts are not likely to be a problem.

Soon after the wedding, however, it becomes apparent that parenting is an important theme for any couple trying to blend two families.

And if their home includes an exceptionally defiant child, then discipline, rules and consequences develop into the dominant aspect of their relationship.

Conflicts naturally arise when one parent views parenting, boundaries and consequences from a different perspective than does their spouse. As we've seen, this problem of differing parenting styles also affects many nuclear families with defiant kids. However, in a nuclear family, the spouses can usually see these differences coming. For years, dating back to when the kids were small, the couple could see that they differed from each other in their views on childrearing; by the time they found themselves struggling with a defiant teen, their differences were not surprising. Extremely irritating, perhaps, but not surprising.

By contrast, in a newly blended family, these differences may be thrust upon the couple with no warning. They have no time to prepare or adjust, as they face substantial discipline issues with an extremely defiant child right off the bat. When faced with this situation, parents in a newly blended family are forced to examine their parenting differences in the raw light of reality. This baptism by fire, so to speak, can be very disheartening to the couple and damaging to the "just beginning to blend" family.

Questions of Loyalty

When factions from two preexisting families attempt to meld together into a new unit, old family loyalties often remain entrenched long after the couple says "I do." These blended families develop what are called "triangles." When I met with a remarried couple the other day, the wife described what happens in their family just this way: "It's like there is this triangle. Me, my husband, and my daughter. I have to be the negotiator between them. I have to explain his actions to her, and I have to plead her case to him. It's exhausting."

The marital relationship is the most important and foundational relationship in any family. Through its cohesiveness and stability, all other family relationships derive their health and strength. As we've mentioned before, a strong, steadfast marital bond is the greatest gift that any parent can give a child. Creating a central marital bond in a blended family, however, can be extremely challenging. In most cases, the old family ties date back years. The parent and child may have lived alone together for a long time before this new relationship began. To go from "it's just you and me, kid, against all-comers" to "I'm always going to side with your stepfather because our solid relationship is the most important aspect of this family" is a formidable task, to say the least. Rearranging the relationships around new lines of loyalty presents an obstacle for many blended families.

Solutions for Blended Families

As we've seen so often, the problems faced by blended families are further complicated by the presence of an extremely defiant child. But each challenge has a practical solution that will help protect your family against internal sabotage.

Avoiding the His-and-Hers Mentality

Choosing parental sides with a his-and-hers mentality is always detrimental to achieving a truly blended family, but the negative effects are magnified when a defiant teen is involved. This parental possessiveness will be exploited by the child, who is already looking for a wedge to divide and conquer his parents. We make it too easy for him when we provide that wedge ourselves. *Mine-and-yours* must shift to *ours* as quickly as possible when it comes to parental responsibilities.

How do you accomplish this? Talk. Talk. And more talk. Preferably, you'll be talking long before an engagement ring is even mentioned. You need to know where this person stands on a multitude of issues, and parenting philosophies should be at the top of that list. Essential topics to cover include how parenting issues, especially those related to the defiant child, will be handled; who will make the decisions; and how each stepparent is expected to relate to their stepchild. It's also vitally important to establish how the parents will make joint parenting decision for all children in the house.

Talking all of these things over prior to any overt commitment may seem obvious. *Of course* a couple is going to talk about all these things and come to a suitable resolution; if they can't, then this union must not be in God's plan and they should move on down the proverbial road, right? Not necessarily. Many people are so afraid of spending the rest of their lives alone that they choose to ignore possible relational disagreements and minimize the potential for future difficulties. Their philosophy seems to be, "This person may not be the best choice, but right now, they are my only choice." It is this mentality that leads second marriages to a divorce rate substantially higher than first marriages. Couples considering remarriage must fully discuss all possible issues, no matter what the outcome may be. If these discussions were not had prior to your marriage, then make the time as soon as possible to ensure that you, as a couple, reach an understanding regarding how your differing roles will begin to be blended . . . starting now.

For couples considering marriage, counseling should be a standard prerequisite. A thorough examination of personal, personality, relational and family-of-origin issues is critical for any couple, but if you already have a child or you're heading to the altar with someone who does, then lengthy prenuptial counseling should be considered mandatory. There are too many issues, too many possible landmines and too many relational variables to take a "love is blind" attitude about marriage. If a person goes into a second marriage without the proper counseling, love isn't blind . . . it's brainless!

Agreeing When Parenting Styles Differ

Agreement begins with dialogue. As is the case with the preceding issue, extensive discussion of parenting styles and past experiences is critical when considering marriage, especially a second marriage. If you know how your parenting views differ, it doesn't mean that you can't get married; it just means that you won't be surprised by the stance your spouse-to-be takes in the future. It also means that you have the opportunity to come to a negotiated understanding.

The key word that unlocks the door to newlywed bliss is *expectations*. Each person brings expectations into a marriage. When those expectations are met, then life is beautiful, the sun shines and animated bluebirds land on your shoulder. But if those expectations are not met, then couples can sometimes be shocked and dismayed by a living arrangement that is not what they bargained for. This can certainly be true of parents with kids who remarry and find their parenting styles do not mesh. Again, just because you may have differing opinions on parenting doesn't mean that you are forbidden to get married; it's just that you need to discuss those differences thoroughly and reach some kind of resolution to avoid future pain and turmoil.

By now, I could ask *you* to identify the most productive method for couples to get on the same page when it comes to parenting choices. I'm certain you would say "a behavior contract." As I've mentioned so many times before, extremely defiant children live to exploit differences and disagreements between parents, and a contract is the most effective weapon I know to defeat this tactic. Long before the ceremony, long before anyone exchanges rings, a clear list of boundaries and a clear list of consequences for stepping over those boundaries should be hammered out and agreed on.

If you didn't do this prior to your marriage, then there is no time like the present to do the right thing. You and your spouse may not agree on all aspects of the parenting process, but you can be in agreement when it comes to the rules and consequences that will govern daily discipline decisions in your home. This unified front will go a long way in reducing the amount of vitriol and discord in your family— *and* in your marriage.

Avoiding Questions of Loyalty

Remember the wife who described her blended family as a "triangle"? She felt trapped in the role of designated intermediary between her husband—the stepfather—and her daughter. This situation had existed for so long that she considered it normal, par for the course in a blended family. Because she introduced geometric formations into the discussion, I thought I'd carry on the imagery. I explained to her that any time she recognized "triangles" in her family, this was a sign of dysfunction. These should be considered red flags pointing to the need for change. A family should not be a triangle with three points but a single, straight line with only two points. In her family triangle, point *A* is the stepdad, point *B* is the mom and point *C* is the stepchild. In other words, the husband and wife represent separate points in the family's relational interactions. If this family was comprised of a straight line, on the other hand, Mom and Stepdad would be a single, unified point *A*, while the stepdaughter would be point *B*. The parents are an inseparable unit to be referred to and treated as if they were not two people, but one. (Hmmm, that sounds almost biblical.)

Stepchildren, particularly exceptionally defiant stepchildren, won't hesitate to exploit divided family loyalties. I hear kids say all the time, "He's not my dad! He can't tell me what to do!" I can understand their point of view, but it happens to be absurd. This childlike logic breaks down rather quickly. The fact that a stepfather, for example, is not a 16-year-old girl's biological dad has nothing to do with her treating him respectfully and complying with his instructions. For example, her math teacher is not her biological father, but she obeys him. The principal of her school is also not her biological father, yet she obeys him. Her basketball coach is not her biological father, but still she obeys him. The examples could go on and on and on. This stepchild may feel sad, hurt, angry and defiant, but those emotions do not give her the right to treat her stepparent any differently than she would treat any other adult authority figure in her life.

What makes defiant children think that they can treat a stepparent differently than other adults who deserve respect? It is that the parents allow them to do so. They overlook disrespectful behavior aimed at the stepparent, in many cases because of continuing guilt over the divorce. In their self-consumed guilt and shame, they assume way too much responsibility for the child's negative behavior. The solution is for fathers and mothers to put aside any guilt they feel about their divorce, along with the resulting pain and turmoil that have touched their children, and bond with their new spouse to present a united front for their children.

There can be no question of loyalty in a blended family. Husbands and wives are loyal to each other first and foremost. And what's equally important is for husbands and wives to communicate this allegiance to their children in no uncertain terms. Remember: You do not abandon your children by pursuing a strong bond with your new spouse; instead, your solid marriage is a beautiful gift that will benefit your children for the rest of their lives.

To Sum It Up

In this chapter, we discussed the special needs that exist in single-parent and blended families. Specifically, we looked at how single parents often feel isolated, are frustrated by a lack of support in their parenting and face ongoing challenges when dealing with an ex-spouse whose approach to parenting does not align with their own.

The solution to the challenges of isolation and a lack of support is to actively seek out family, friends or support groups that can give guidance, offer a fresh perspective and maybe even give parents a break when they feel overwhelmed by the stresses of dealing with a defiant child. To avoid ex-spouse issues, single parents are urged to agree on a behavior contract that can be implemented in both households. If coming to agreement just isn't practical, given the level of discord, parents need to accept their inability to change an ex-spouse who is aggressively working against their parenting choices. Instead of focusing on what they can't control, they can focus on their own spiritual health and work to make proper, healthy parenting choices in whatever areas they have opportunity.

We then looked at some of the special issues faced by blended families, including the problem created by a his-and-hers parenting strategy, by differing parenting styles and by old lines of loyalty dividing the blended family.

To avoid developing a his-and-hers mentality, a couple must enter the relationship with a purposeful plan to maintain shared responsibilities. They must see all children in their family as *ours*, and they must approach family discipline as a joint endeavor. Again, a behavior contract is the most helpful tool for helping the newly formed couple work from the same page when it comes to parenting decisions. By presenting a united front, they take away much of the ammunition used against them by the exceptionally defiant child. Finally, to avoid questions of loyalty, parents must overcome guilty feelings about their divorce and make sure that they communicate to their kids that the new husband and wife are a solidified unit and will act that way in all family interactions—especially in discipline and parenting issues.

A Quick Follow-up

You'll remember Amy and Jason as the blended family who had divided up the parenting responsibilities between which kids were his and which kids were hers. This philosophy caused unneeded stress in both their marriage and in the family as a whole. I was pleased to see their eagerness to examine this problem from a new perspective, and to see their openness to approaching the issue from a different angle. They soon saw the need for the primacy of their marital relationship within the family, and worked very hard to present a united front to all of their children. A contract was implemented, and both parents enforced it for all the children living in the house. One parent was not more or less in authority than the other regarding the behavior of any of the children, no matter who the biological parent might have been. It took some time, but things were improving for Amy and Jason when last I saw them.

IF YOU'RE A SINGLE PARENT, HAVE A SEAT ON THE COUCH

1. Have you experienced feelings of isolation as a single parent with a defiant child? What most often triggers those feelings?

2. Have you found it difficult to get support for dealing with your extremely defiant child? Is it that people just don't understand, or would you attribute it to some other issue? Explain your answer.

3. If you and your ex-spouse agree about most parenting issues, do you think a contract could be implemented in both homes? Why or why not?

4. If you and your ex-spouse disagree about parenting issues, can you accept the fact that you can't change the negative influence of your ex-spouse? How would recognizing this reality change your perspective on parenting?

IF YOU'RE A PARENT IN A BLENDED FAMILY, HAVE A SEAT ON THE COUCH

1. Have you and your spouse ever struggled with the his-and-hers mentality? If so, what form did it take? If not, how do you think you were able to avoid it?

2. If you and your spouse's parenting style are substantially different, how have you made that work in your blended family? Do you think a contract would be helpful? Explain your answer.

3. Do you believe that there are loyalty issues within your blended family? What evidence do you see to support your answer?

4. Do you feel continuing guilt over putting your children through a divorce? How have you dealt with that guilt? Do you think that it has ever led to inappropriate parenting decisions? How will you apply what you learned in this chapter to make different decisions in the future?

I'M SO GLAD WE'VE HAD THIS TIME TOGETHER

We got a new football coach for my senior year of high school, and I remember the first day he called us all into the locker room to share with us that things were going to be slightly different under his watch. He informed us that there would be a zero-tolerance policy when it came to drugs or alcohol; that if your grades were not passing, then you wouldn't be allowed to play until they were; and finally, that your hair had to be off the collar in the back and above the ears on the side.

Now, I agreed with him on all of his policy initiatives until it came to the last one. This was 1977, after all, and I had a head of hair that would have made Tony Orlando blush, and a pair of pork-chop sideburns that would have made Elvis proud.

But here is how the coach communicated these new rules: "Now, fellas, you can still drink if you want to. You can have hair down to your rear end if that's what you want to do, and you know what? I'll still be your friend . . . but you won't be able to play on this team. You can have all the failing grades you want, and we'll still be good friends . . . it's just that you will not be able to be a part of this team."

This form of authority made a profound impact on me. I remember thinking how cool it was that this person in authority over me could disagree with me but still consider me his friend. Later, as a young parent, I remember thinking that this approach could apply to parenting our kids as well—that, as a parent, I didn't have to be angry or domineering to have and enforce firm boundaries in our home. Anger and discipline were not, and should not be, bound together. They were completely separate.

Hopefully, you have understood this as one of the central themes of this book. I pray that in some small way, this discussion we've had will help alleviate some of the anger in your home and make room for the peace God promises to all His children.

As we come to the close of our time together, I want you to know how much I appreciate what you are trying to do. As Paul told young Timothy, "I have fought the good fight, I have finished the race, I have kept the faith" (2 Tim. 4:7). Your decision to read this book tells me that you are in the midst of fighting the good fight, and I want to assure you that your heavenly Father knows the struggle you are enduring to reconcile your defiant teen back to Him. I know the struggle you wake up into every day, and I pray that you will never feel alone when you consider His promise to always be with you.

Below, you will find seven days of peace and promise from your heavenly Father. Make these Scriptures and prayerful meditations a regular part of your prayer life. Memorize these verses so that the Holy Spirit can bring them to your mind in times of need. Pray through these thoughts each day so that you can focus your mind on what is important, instead of simply on what is urgent.

If you don't yet have a daily time alone with the Lord, then this is a perfect time to start one. Realistically, we cannot ask Him for support and guidance if we are not going to take the time to listen to His response. As the parent of a defiant teenager, you need to establish a daily one on one time with God so that His Word can become the source of your courage and strength. But you can't hear those words if you don't stop to listen.

This book is all about committing to make a change in the following areas of your life:

- The way you view the parenting process
- The way you interact with your spouse
- The way you handle the discipline in your home
- The way you understand your child's defiant behavior
- The way you understand your own emotional makeup

But, most importantly, I hope this book has challenged you reexamine your relationship with God. If you are reading this and you are not a Christian, I pray that you will seek Him with all your heart, because the Bible promises that if you do, you will find Him. The peace, comfort, guidance and support from Christ that we've been talking about can be yours by simply opening your heart to Him. Remember when we said that this struggle with your defiant child may have more of a purpose for you than for your child? Well, I could not imagine a more powerful purpose than for you to experience the love, forgiveness and redemption that come with a relationship with Christ.

If you are a believer, then I hope you've been encouraged to deny yourself, take up your cross and follow Him (see Matt. 16:24). Make these verses and prayer thoughts a vital part of your daily walk with Him.

Seven Days of Peace and Promise for Parents of Defiant Kids

I would like for all of us to claim the promise of Psalm 119:105: "Your word is a lamp to my feet and a light to my path." God's Word is full of promises that show us the Way of life—promises that have stood unmoved for thousands of years. I encourage you who are a parent of an exceptionally defiant teen to grab hold of these promises and hold on to them for dear life. Within these verses are life, and a promise of hope for you, no matter what your family circumstance may be.

Below, you will find one promise from your heavenly Father that you can claim for each day of the week. Read them each day, meditate on them and incorporate them into your life. This is the way to have God's Word live in you. And once you have His Word living in you, a world of opportunities await. As Jesus promised: "If you remain in me and my words remain in you, ask whatever you wish, and it will be given you" (John 15:7). Do you want to pack a punch in your prayer life? Well, this is the way to do it.

Monday's Promise for You: Galatians 2:20

I have been crucified with Christ and I no longer live, but Christ lives in me. The life I live in the body, I live by faith in the Son of God, who loved me and gave himself for me.

Pray today that you will allow Jesus Himself to flow through you. Pray each day to empty yourself out and allow the Holy Spirit to fill you up. Let Him, *through you*, impact every decision you make and every relationship you engage in today.

Tuesday's Promise for You: Psalm 23:4

Even though I walk through the valley of the shadow of death, I will fear no evil, for you are with me; your rod and your staff, they comfort me.

Pray today to experience reassurance from God. He never promised that He would keep you out of the valley, just that He would walk right by your side all the way through. No matter what trauma or time of turmoil you may be experiencing, God's promise is that He will be right there with you. He will never abandon you or forsake you.

Wednesday's Promise for You: Philippians 4:13

I can do everything through him who gives me strength.

Pray today that you will realize that there is no hardship, no conflict, no difficult circumstance that you cannot overcome—not because you're so great and wonderful, but because God gives you the strength to do it. Christ in you is your hope. Christ in you is your strength.

Thursday's Promise for You: 1 Samuel 17:45-47

David said to the Philistine, "You come against me with sword and spear and javelin, but I come against you in the name of the LORD Almighty, the God of the armies of Israel, whom you have defied. This day the LORD will hand you over to me, and I'll strike you down and cut off your head. Today I will give the carcasses of the Philistine army to the birds of the air and the beasts of the earth, and the whole world will know that there is a God in Israel. All those gathered here will know that it is not by sword or spear that the LORD saves; for the battle is the LORD's, and he will give all of you into our hands."

Wow, I get excited just typing this one out! Pray today that no matter how big your giant is, no matter how hopeless your circumstance may appear and no matter how discouraging your situation seems, God will deliver you—because your battle is God's battle, and you *will* have victory in it, if for no other reason than to show the whole world that there is a God in your family!

Friday's Promise for You: Philippians 1:6

Being confident of this, that he who began a good work in you will carry it on to completion until the day of Christ Jesus.

Pray today that you will be encouraged knowing that God didn't build His home in you to move away. He didn't bless you with this family only to see Satan tear it down. Know that there is purpose to this pain. Remember that to purify gold, it takes a fire. He will complete the work that He started in you and your family.

Saturday's Promise for You: Galatians 5:22-23

But the fruit of the Spirit is love, joy, peace, patience, kindness, goodness, faithfulness, gentleness and self-control. Against such things there is no law.

Pray today that you will allow the presence of the Holy Spirit to flow through you to express all of these attributes. These characteristics are to show through the life of the believer no matter what their circumstances. Try to find times today when you can express these fruits to those whom God brings into your sphere of influence, especially your defiant teen.

Sunday's Promise for You: Joshua 24:14-15

Now fear the LORD and serve him with all faithfulness. Throw away the gods your forefathers worshiped beyond the River and in Egypt, and serve the LORD. But if serving the LORD seems undesirable to you, then choose for yourselves this day whom you will serve, whether the gods your forefathers served beyond the River, or the gods of the Amorites, in whose land you are living. But as for me and my household, we will serve the LORD.

Take every Lord's Day to claim your family for God. Choose this Lord's Day to put Christ first in every aspect of your family's life, no matter what anyone else is doing or whether anyone else agrees.

We Need to Stop the Silence

As I mentioned at the beginning, one of the motivating factors that led to the writing of this book was the fact that so many of my clients feel as though they are the only Christian parents that are grappling with an extremely defiant teenager. Surely there must be something wrong with them as parents or as believers for their families to be struggling with a defiant child like theirs.

A distraught mother came into my office this week, overcome with guilt and hopelessness when she explained to me her family circumstance. Her son was extremely defiant; he was verbally and physically abusive at home and had already had several run ins with law enforcement—and he was only 15 years old. The woman's husband didn't want her to be here, because he felt that they could handle their rebellious child on their own. He didn't feel as though the son's actions and attitudes were much to be concerned about, and that his wife was making a mountain out of a molehill. But what caused her the most discouragement was the fact that they were a very committed Christian family who went to church all the time and tried hard to instill biblical values in their children. With tears in her eyes, she said, "I can't believe this is happening to us. If all our church friends knew what was going on in our home, they would think we are such hypocrites. We must be the worst Christian parents in the world." This woman felt lost and all alone.

Hopefully by now, you understand that this is not the case. Tens of thousands of Christian homes around the country struggle with an extremely defiant child. Yet most of these tens of thousands of parents seems to think that they are the only ones who have this problem. We need to stop the silence.

I suggest that you take matters into your own hands in this matter. Be proactive in your attempts to find others with whom you can share your common stories and from whom you can receive encouragement and support. The following are a couple of ways that you can do this.

Form a Local Group

Contact your church's pastor or youth minister about getting a support group started for parents who have difficult kids. If you feel that this is too narrow of an approach, then begin a weekly or monthly parent group, open to all parents, to discuss all sorts of parenting issues. You might even suggest an anonymous survey for the parents of the teens in your church's youth group to see if they are interested in a group of this sort. Volunteer to help facilitate and organize the group, offer the use of your home if a church room is not available, volunteer to publicize the group and offer to gather discussion materials for use during the meetings.

Have you noticed the tactic here? Take it from a long-time church staff minister: The last thing those on staff at your church will want to do is take on the responsibility of leading another group. Most of the ministers on staff at your church are just about "meetinged-out." So try and take away most, if not all, of the objections that they may offer to the formation of this group before they have the chance to say anything negative.

Another great source of support, education and encouragement might be to form a parents-of-teens Bible study class at your church. This group would meet when all the other Bible study groups meet for your church, whether on Sunday mornings, Sunday nights or some other evening during the week. I have led a parenting Sunday school class at my church for years, and find it to be a rewarding and beneficial experiences for me and for those who attend. In your class, you may have parents with small kids learning from those more experienced, younger parents who give new insights and perspectives to older ones or parents with defiant children who can gain support, empathy and insight from the others in the room. It is a powerful experience when one set of parents shares a particular struggle and have other parents join together to pray for them and for their family.

I see your church family as the most viable choice for getting hurting parents together, but you could take the same approach with your kid's school or homeschool co-op. Ask the principal if a group like this might not be a wonderful resource for the school to provide for parents. Again, you'll have to be the initiator and motivator, but all that many churches or schools need to make this dream a reality is a layperson to take the bull by the horns.

Wherever you can get parents together and talking, you will be amazed to find that parents in your community, neighborhood or church are struggling with the same issues that you are. Why don't you be the instrument in God's hands to bring each of these hurting families together?

Form a Group Online

Let's put the Internet to a greater use than being a conduit for pornography to our homes. Try initiating an online discussion forum for Christian parents with extremely defiant kids on an Internet discussion board. Discussion boards of this kind can be found on many online sites such as Yahoo, MSN, AOL and others.

On a personal note, The Timothy Center, the adolescent Christian counseling center where I work here in Austin, has instituted just such a discussion forum. We have parents from all over the country who sign in anonymously to discuss their situations and seek guidance and support from other Christian parents going through the same situation. This particular forum has been operating for about a year now, and we are very pleased with the results.

Whatever option you choose, just choose one and get started breaking the silence. Be proactive in changing the present cultural environment, which seems to ignore the needs of Christian families who battle with defiant kids in their homes.

My Prayer for You

As you work hard to turn your defiant child toward the Son, and commit your family to your Lord every day, know that this is my prayer for you:

I pray that you will always see the good in your child,
and that you will focus on his potential as much as on his failings.
I pray that, if you're married, you and your spouse will truly be one—
what God has joined together, let no one separate.
I pray that, if you're a single parent, your relationship with Christ
will be all-sufficient for you.
I pray that you will find a source of comfort and peace
in a renewed relationship with your heavenly Father,
and that His words will renew you day by day,
giving you strength and direction from above.
I pray that the Lord Jesus Christ will heal your child, your family and
your heart.
And I pray that God will use your home to be a beacon of His light
in the midst of this very dark world.

APPENDIX

SAMPLE BEHAVIOR CONTRACT

On the following pages is a sample behavior contract. This is not an exhaustive document; rather, it's a simplified example of what you can develop for your home. There are many appropriate rules and conduct expectations not listed here that should be included on your contract. You'll notice that it is designed to be very simple and forthright. The idea is to get your family's contract down to no more two pages, which can then be laminated and hung on the refrigerator. This makes for easy access when tenants of the contract may be in dispute. And trust me, they *will* be in dispute.

There are two columns. One column is for expectations and the other is for consequences that will result if those expectations are not met. At the end of the contract is a section for an overall explanation of the document and any other information that needs to be addressed.

Remember: You know your child better than anyone. What you include on your contract will be determined by your child's age, the specific behavior areas that need to be addressed for your child and the rules and expectations specific to your family.

BEHAVIOR CONTRACT

Home Conduct

WHAT WE EXPECT	AND IF YOU DON'T
1. You will not act disrespectfully to your parents. This means no raising your voice, no disrespectful comments and no physical touching in anger.	See Disrespect
2. You will not leave the house without permission from one of your parents, and at least one parent will know where you are at all times.	See Disobedience
3. You will always tell the truth. This means that if we think you're not telling the truth, you will receive the consequence. Parents do not have to prove that you are lying.	See Dishonesty

Home Rules

WHAT WE EXPECT	AND IF YOU DON'T
1. In bed by 10 PM. This means that lights are off and no electronic media is on.	See Disobedience
2. You will be off your cell phone at 9 PM.	See Disobedience

Home Rules–Continued

WHAT WE EXPECT	AND IF YOU DON'T
3. You will be up and ready for school by 7 AM. This means you're completely ready, including having eaten breakfast.	See Disobedience

School Conduct and Grades

WHAT WE EXPECT	AND IF YOU DON'T
1. You will receive no more that one conduct referral per semester.	See Disobedience
2. You will receive no less than a B on a report card unless the situation has been previously discussed with a parent.	See Disobedience

Consequences

Disobedience

You will loose all electronic devices (if it has batteries, a screen or plugs in, it is included) for 48 hours. Parents will set the time this countdown begins.

Dishonesty

You will loose all electronics for 48 hours and will be grounded to the house during the next weekend. This time begins after school on Friday and continues through bedtime Sunday night.

Disrespect

You will be on total Lock Down for a full 72 hours. This includes no electronics, no leaving the house, no one coming to the house and no communication with anyone outside the family.

Additional Information

1. These consequences are just the starting point. If behavior does not improve with the consequences at this level, they will be increased.

2. It is important that everyone familiarize themselves with this contract, because everyone will be held accountable to its content. Ignorance of the law is no excuse.

3. **Remember:** If you act in a disrespectful manner during the implementation of the contract, consequences will be doubled.

Final Consequence

This contract is our attempt, as your parents, to instill in you a sense of personal responsibility and respectable conduct. If this contract fails to amend your behavior, then *you* will be choosing to remove yourself from this home. You must know that we love you and will go to great lengths to keep you in our home, but if negative and defiant behavior continues, then *you* will be choosing no longer to live in this house. We would never kick you out of this house—this is your home—but you can choose *not* to live here. And by not complying with the expectations of this contract, you will be making that choice.

ENDNOTES

Introduction: Winning the War on Terror
1. Douglas Riley, *The Defiant Child: A Parent's Guide to Oppositional Defiant Disorder* (Lanham, MD: Taylor Trade Publishing, 1997), p. 3.
2. One note: Some children's aberrant behavior may be the result of a more serious psychological disorder like major depressive disorder, bipolar disorder, or some type of anxiety disorder. Any time you see a pattern of prolonged negative behavior in your child that seems to be outside the norm of other adolescent behavior, I strongly suggest that you seek input from a medical doctor or licensed professional counselor in your area.

Chapter 1: It's Never Too Late
1. Eduardo M. Bustamante, *Treating the Disruptive Adolescent: Finding the Real Self Behind Oppositional Defiant Disorders* (Northvale, NJ: Jason Aronson, Inc., 2000), p. 21.

Chapter 2: So When Do We Start to Worry?
1. R. A. Barkley and C. M. Benton, *Your Defiant Child: Eight Steps to Better Behavior*, (New York, NY: Guilford Press, 1998), p. 10.
2. W. G. Ross, *The Explosive Child: A New Approach for Understanding and Parenting Easily Frustrated, Chronically Inflexible Children* (New York, NY: HarperCollins, 1998), p. 12.
3. Robert Shaw, *The Epidemic: The Rot of American Culture, Absentee and Permissive Parenting, and the Resultant Plague of Joyless, Selfish Children* (New York, NY: Regan Books, 2003), p. 15.
4. Robert McGee, *Search For Significance: Seeing Your True Worth Through God's Eyes* (Nashville, TN: Thomas Nelson, 1998), p. 27.
5. Ibid., p. 30.
6. Melody Green, "Make My Life a Prayer" (New York, NY: EMI April Music, Inc.).

Chapter 3: Rules Without a Relationship
1. W. Oscar Thompson, Jr., Claude V. King and Carolyn Thompson Ritzmann *Concentric Circles of Concern: Seven Stages for Making Disciples* (Nashville, TN: B&H Publishing Group, 2nd rev. ed., 1999), p. 8.
2. Christopher Maag, "A Hoax Turned Fatal Draws Anger But No Charges," *The New York Times*, November 28, 2007. http://www.nytimes.com/2007/11/28/us/28hoax.html (accessed March 2009).
3. Chap Clark and Dee Clark, *Disconnected: Parenting Teens in a MySpace World* (Grand Rapids, MI: Baker Books, 2008), p. 66.
4. Winston Churchill, "Never Give In, Never, Never, Never," speech delivered at Harrow School on October 29, 1941. http://www.winstonchurchill.org/i4a/pages/index.cfm?pageid=423 (accessed March 2009).

Chapter 4: The Question of Control
1. Dietrich Bonhoeffer, *The Cost of Discipleship* (New York, NY: Touchstone, 1995), p. 45.

Chapter 5: If We Keep Doing the Same Things the Same Way . . .
1. Dr. Seuss, *Horton Hatches the Egg* (New York, NY: Random House, 1940), p. 21.
2. Rick Warren, *The Purpose-Driven Life: What On Earth Am I Here For?* (Grand Rapids, MI: Zondervan, 2002), p. 17.

Chapter 7: Your Secret Weapon
1. R. Wolkomir and J. Wolkomir, "Mr. Edison Takes a Holiday," *Smithsonian*, December 1999, pp. 136-149.

Chapter 8: The Great Consequences Debate

1. "Consequence," *The American Heritage Dictionary of the English Language, Fourth Edition* (New York, NY: Houghton Mifflin Company, 2006).

Chapter 9: Don't Let Your Marriage Become Collateral Damage

1. J. K. Myers, *Understanding the Influences of Parenting a Child with Oppositional Defiant Disorder on the Marital Relationship: A Phenomenological Study* (Ann Arbor, MI: Pro Quest, 2007), p. 8.

Chapter 10: Special Focus: Single-parent and Blended Families

1. L. D. Krauth, "Single-parent Families: The Risk to Children," *Family Therapy News,* December 1995, 26(6), p. 14.
2. R. Garfield, "Mourning and Its Resolution for Spouses in Marital Separation, from J. C. Hansen and L. Messinger, Editors, *Therapy with Remarriage Families* (Rockville, MD: Aspen, 1982) pp. 1-16.
3. L. D. Krauth, "Single-parent Families," p. 14.
4. M. Elias, "Parenting Turns Men's Lives on End, *USA Today,* June 19-21, 1992, pp. 1A-2A.
5. S. A. Levitan and E. A. Conway, "Families in Flux," (Washington, DC: Bureau of National Affairs, 1990) p. 77.
6. G. G. Barnes, "Divorce Transitions: Identifying Risk and Promoting Resilience for Children and Their Parental Relationship," *Journal of Marital and Family Therapy,* 1999, 25, pp. 425-441.
7. P. C. Glick, "A Demographic Perspective of Stepfamilies," Address to the annual conference of the Stepfamily Association of America, Lincoln, NE, October 1991.
8. W. L. MacDonald and A. DeMaris, "Parenting Stepchildren and Biological Children: The Effects of Stepparent's Gender and New Biological Children, *Journal of Family Issues,* 1996, 17, pp. 5-25.
9. L. Nielson, "Stepmothers: Why So Much Stress?" *Journal of Divorce and Remarriage,* 1999, 30(1/2), pp. 115-148.
10. P. Papernow, quoted in *Normal Family Processes,* 3rd edition, edited by Froma Walsh (New York: The Guiliford Press, 2002).

GIVE THANKS . . .

I would like to thank . . .

Sarah, Josh and Lindsey for being my example and inspiration.

Bob and Ruth Lindsey for your never-ending love and support.

Steve and Roxanne for sharing the vision before there was a vision.

Billy, Margaret and Jennifer for giving me your insight and professional expertise.

Laura Barker for helping me say what is truly on my heart.

Jane Gibson for your spirit of service and giving, and for your artistic eye.

Mike Cooper and WORDSearch™—I truly don't know how I could do what I do without you (www.wordsearchbible.com).

Kim Bangs at Regal for taking a chance on an unpublished newbie.

Bucky Rosenbaum for believing.

ABOUT THE AUTHOR

Dr. Jimmy Myers is the director of The Timothy Center, a Christian counseling center in Austin, Texas, which specializes in working with adolescents and their families. For more information about The Timothy Center, visit **www.timothycenter.com**. If you would like to log on to the Parent Forum, where you can interact with other Christian parents of defiant teens from around the country, you can access that page from The Timothy Center's website.

To communicate with Dr. Myers, check out where he may be speaking in your area, read his blog or purchase additional copies of *Toe to Toe with Your Teen*, log on to **www.jimmymyers.com**. For more information or to schedule a speaking engagement, you can email Dr. Myers at **info@jimmymyers.com** or contact him at the following:

Family Faith Ministries
11754 Jollyville Rd. #110
Austin, Texas 78759
(512)-705-2067